The Katy Perry Album

Mick O'Shea

Plexus, London

Contents

The Girl From Goleta

'Santa Barbara is my hood. I mean, it's not much of a hood, but it is definitely like my hood. I claim Santa Barbara like I claim my family – I'm going to be married and buried there.'

Though it may seem odd that someone whose parents were both pastors, who attended Christian schools and summer camps, sang in her local church, and whose debut album was made up entirely of gospel songs, should subsequently pen risqué ditties such as 'Ur So Gay', and 'I Kissed A Girl', Katy Perry has plenty of famous musical forebears who came from similarly Bible-thumping households to take the pop world by storm. Of course, Elvis Presley, Little Richard, Jerry Lee Lewis, Buddy Holly, and those other early rock'n'roll pioneers, were raised on a strict musical diet of Gospel music because they all came from God-fearing Southern American states, where, somewhat ironically, rock'n'roll would be – and probably still is – regarded as the devil's music.

More modern-day examples are found in Guns N' Roses frontman, Axl Rose, Nirvana's Kurt Cobain, Alanis Morissette, and Avril Lavigne. In Katy's case, however, although her parents had turned away from 'secular music', rock'n'roll was definitely in the blood.

Katy was born Katheryn Elizabeth Hudson on 25 October 1984, to Keith and Mary Hudson in Santa Barbara, California. Back in the 1960s, her Memphis-born dad Keith, having fled his native Tennessee, took the hippie trail to sunny California to become a West Coast scenester and 'turned on, tuned in and dropped out' with counter-culture drug guru Timothy Leary. It was here that he encountered the nomadic Mary Perry, a Southern Californian native of mixed race who'd recently returned from Zimbabwe following the collapse of her marriage. Mary was an equally free spirit who'd embraced everything the 1960s had to offer, and had at one time dated legendary guitarist Jimi Hendrix. But both had given up living life in the fast lane in favour of serving God by the time Katy's older sister Angela entered the world. 'My mother used to hang out with Jimi Hendrix, and my father sold acid called Strawberry Fields for Timothy Leary,' Katy told *The Mirror*. 'Even though my mum isn't a wild child rock'n'roller, pot-smoking debutante that she was, and my dad isn't the acid dealer with long

Katy poses for photographers during a visit to MTV's Total Request Live studios in New York.

hair anymore, they've probably had more intense moments than anything I've ever done.'

But while Katy is happy to speak about her parents' former happy-go-lucky hippie lifestyle, she is also quick to point out that they might not have survived the trip had it not been for their finding religion. As she told *The Daily Telegraph*: 'Dad would have died from one tab too many. They both had a wild life, then they found God and felt like they needed to have a personal change, and that's how they decided to raise me.'

But their parents' hedonistic past didn't mean that Angela, Katy, and younger brother Daniel were allowed free rein during their formative years. Like most people who pull themselves back from the edge of their own self-indulgences, Keith and Mary were resolute in their determination that their offspring wouldn't succumb to similar temptation. 'I knew about hell from the moment I understood a sentence,' Katy told *Rolling Stone*. 'I had fuzzy-felt boards with Satan and people gnashing their teeth. My religious upbringing was comically strict – even the Dirt Devil vacuum cleaner was banned. In our house, no one was allowed to refer to deviled eggs. We had to call them "angelic eggs". We were never allowed to swear. I'd get into trouble just for saying, "Hell, no!" If you dropped a hammer on your toe in our house, you had to say something like, "Jiminy Christmas." I wasn't even able to say I was lucky because my mom would rather us say that we were blessed, and she also didn't like that lucky sounded like Lucifer. I wasn't allowed to eat Lucky Charms, but I think that was the sugar. I think my mom lied to me on that one.'

'I was a hyperactive kid, and my mom and dad got used to me creating a stir. Whether we were on holiday, or eating around the dining table, I would always come up with something outrageous.' – Katy Perry

Until Katy reached the age of three, the Hudsons lived in the coastal village of Goleta, which lay a few miles further along the coast from Santa Barbara. But Katy's idyllic life of sun, sea and sand came to an abrupt end when her preacher parents uprooted the family to embark on a state-by-state tour of the country, with the aim of setting up an evangelical church wherever they stopped off long enough to call home. 'We lived in two different places in Oklahoma, then two places in Arizona and then Florida for a while,' she recounted for *Rolling Stone*. 'Then back to Santa Barbara – you can take a breath now! I think at the time it affected me emotionally because I had to leave friends like the ones I left behind. But looking back, I got to make a lot of friends, see a lot of places and take a little bit of everywhere with me.'

But while her parents' evangelical wanderings across America in search of those in need of salvation allowed Katy and her siblings to sample experiences that might otherwise have been denied them – not to mention give them an excellent grounding in geography – their nomadic existence in the service of the Lord did have its drawbacks. What food was available would more often than not be shared with their congregation, and essentials such as healthcare were luxuries the Hudsons had to forego.

Of course, it wasn't until later that Katy learnt of her parents' wayward past, but while she was happy to embrace their devotion to God, she must have wondered why the other kids in the neighbourhood were able to watch MTV and listen to what her mother referred to as 'secular music'. As she later told the music channel: 'I was raised in a very pseudo-religious household where the only thing on the menu was gospel standards like "Oh Happy Day", "His Eye Is On The Sparrow" and "Amazing Grace" – all eight verses of it. There was only

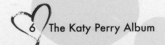

*Left: Little Katy Hudson, long before she was famous. **Right**: Katy's high-school yearbook photo.*

church; church friends, church school, and of course, actual church. I thought it was normal at the time, but it wasn't. I could only go to the movies if they reviewed it first. They let me see anything with a remnant of God – *Sister Act 2*, *The Preacher's Wife*, that kinda thing.'

One secular songstress who slipped through the net was Alanis Morissette. '*Jagged Little Pill* was huge for me,' Katy later confessed to *Prefix* magazine. 'One of the vivid memories of my childhood is swinging on the swing set singing "Ironic" [released as the fourth single from *Jagged Little Pill* in February 1996] at the top of my lungs. I went to a Christian school, so I got into a little trouble for that one.'

In accordance with her parents' beliefs, every summer Katy and her sister Angela would be packed off to summer camp for further religious instruction. The primary purpose of summer camp is for educational and cultural development, but in 2006, the documentary *Jesus Camp*, which received a 'Best Documentary Feature' nomination at that year's Oscars, lifted the lid on the strict disciplines at the Kids On Fire School of Ministry, a Pentecostal Charismatic Christian summer camp located just outside Devil's Lake, North Dakota, where kids as young as five were being groomed as miniature warriors to 'take back America for Christ'. And though the filmmakers attempted to create an objective documentary, the ensuing reaction from the general public resulted in the camp's closure later that same year.

'I watched it [*Jesus Camp*],' Katy told *CBS News*. 'And I was like, "Oh, my God! I didn't know they had behind the scenes footage of my childhood!"'

Despite the Hudsons' self-imposed life of near-Puritan austerity, by her own admission

Katy was a bit of a tomboy. 'I spent all day at the skateboard park with a friend of mine who was so good that she ended up going pro,' she said. 'I wasn't quite so good, but I could easily handle a half-pipe, when you're skating almost vertically. I gave up because I was scuffing my knees so much and I didn't like the idea of breaking bones.'

She would also lay claim to being something of an unruly child: 'I was a hyperactive kid, and my mom and dad got used to me creating a stir,' she reflected. 'Whether we were on holiday, or eating around the dining table, I would always come up with something outrageous.'

This, however, sounds like Katy's wishful thinking; her need to feel that she enjoyed an ordinary childhood, and that she got up to all the usual kinds of mischief that kids get up to. Because her parents' abstemious lifestyle would surely have meant that the usual avenues for self-expression would have been denied her. And yet, though vanity was considered one of the seven deadly sins, her mother raised no objections when Katy expressed an interest in child beauty pageants; the spectacle which extols the wilful sexualisation of prepubescent girls that is peculiar to America. (The pageants, which already had a growing number of detractors, would come under intense scrutiny following the abduction and murder of six-year-old JonBenét Ramsey in 1996.)

'My hourglass shape is probably my best feature. I play off of that a lot. I like that I have a lot on top, and a lot on the bottom.' – Katy Perry

At the time, the Hudsons were living in Lake Havasu, Arizona, and Katy's mother – not averse to the idea of a little extra attention – entered Katy into a mini-pageant staged at the local grocery store.

Katy would later blog: 'It wasn't a hard race – just between a couple of other girls at the store.' Despite the low turnout, Katy would have to settle for 'measly' second place. And the runner-up spot was to be her reward when she subsequently competed in a national pageant – regardless of her fetching pink satin suit and matching bowler hat. 'I got second place [again],' she bemoaned on her blog. 'SECOND PLACE IS NOT GOOD ENOUGH . . . I bet it was because mom cut corners.'

And though she was to be denied the pageant crown in her own right, she hasn't given up on basking in its reflected glory: 'Okay, maybe there's an age restriction. That's fine; I'll just become a pageant mom. I'm sure there's room for two pageant bitches. Soft curls, fake lashes, [Swarovski] crystals, and a big smile, welcome to your "Little Miss Perfect" addiction.'

Another childhood obsession of Katy's was her body. Her mother had curves, and her sister Angela was showing signs of maturity, yet she herself had nothing. And such was her longing for big boobs that at the tender age of nine she took to calling on help from above. 'I remember kneeling by my bed, saying my prayers and asking God to give me boobs that were so big that if I laid on my back, I wouldn't be able to see my feet,' she confessed to *Blender* magazine. But it must have seemed a classic case of 'be careful what you wish for', as by the time she was thirteen her breasts were rapidly outgrowing the rest of her. 'I had real back problems,' she added wistfully. 'Then I grew up and lost the baby fat and said, "Hey, this isn't all that bad." Besides my big boobs, it is probably my hourglass shape that is my best feature. I play off of that a lot. I like that I have a lot on top, and a lot on the bottom.'

Katy adopts a punkette look at
a launch party for Nintendo DS.

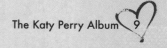

2

It's Okay To Believe

'Maybe you're [the] reason why all the doors are closed, so you can open one that leads you to the perfect road.'

Though her cutesy image failed to grab the main pageantry prize, it wasn't long before Katy discovered her talent for singing was beginning to garner attention. 'When I would sing, people's faces would light up,' she later told *The Oregonian*. 'It was my only magic trick.'

However, it wasn't so much a magic trick as a twist of fate that would inadvertently set Katy on her path. Like most young girls with an older female sibling, Katy diligently copied everything Angela did, and it was happening upon one of her sister's cassette tapes, featuring a selection of songs by the contemporary Christian singer Carman (Domenic Licciardello), which would offer a boost to her burgeoning gifts. 'I picked up a Carman track. That's honest. "River Of Life" by Carman,' she told *Christian Music Central*. 'That's all I ever grew up on, Christian music. I picked it up because my sister started singing and I copied every little thing she did. It was actually her tape, but I stole it. So I took it, and I practiced and I performed it before she did.'

Though she herself was reticent about taking her vocal talents further than singing in front of her bedroom mirror, she was ever eager to shine in her parents' eyes, and jumped at the chance when they suggested she seek lessons with a vocal coach to improve her voice. 'Mom was actually the first one to get me involved in this,' she told *Christian Retailing*. 'She threw me off the edge because she's a total stage mom! Then I came back and realised this is what I want to do, not what my parents want me to do.'

She added: 'My mom would take me when I was eleven or so and we'd do [concerts at] weekend churches. I didn't want to be there because I wanted to be eleven. I wanted to do what you [the average kid] do at eleven. But then I saw how I affected and touched people [with my voice].'

Bolstered by her parents' encouragement – coupled with the ten dollars her dad would give her every time she got up to sing – she began performing in church, as well as at various family functions. She was also happy to do impromptu birthday requests at local restaurants, and would serenade a table with the latest gospel tune.

Katy poses in the press room after the 2010 Grammy nominations – her single
'Hot N Cold' was nominated for Best Female Pop Vocal Performance.

A fresh-faced Katy attends an MTV-sponsored red-carpet event.

'Wherever I went, restaurants or whatever, I would get up and sing "Amazing Grace",' she said. 'Not that I was one of those stage kids. There was no JonBenét Ramsey inside of me waiting to burst out. I just started. . . writing little songs about God, or this boy I liked; the two men in my life at the same time.'

Her constantly being lavished with praise meant that her ego took something of a nosedive upon enrolling for music lessons at the Santa Barbara Christian School and realising there were others who were more musically gifted. But rather than duck into her shell, the competition merely spurred her on. 'Katy was part of a large class which just happened to be full of leaders, people who are extremely talented and are looking for attention and leadership,' said her tutor, Nathan Kreitzer. 'She was already a talented vocalist when she was in my classes. She was rebellious but, to be fair, those kids who are destined to do great things tend to be agitators.'

The class may well have been brimming with prodigious talents, but Katy – like the proverbial cream – slowly yet effortlessly rose to the top.

But while Katy no doubt relished her reputation for being considered risqué within the insular corridors of a religious school, she was reduced to a wide-eyed innocent on her first day at Dos Pueblos, a secular secondary high school located in El Encanto Heights in Goleta. She found herself facing something of a paradox, because these were the kids her parents had thus far sheltered her from, yet though initially wary, she found their *joie de vivre* highly intoxicating. 'When I faced public high school, I didn't exclude myself from the worldly kids,' she told *Christian Music Central*. 'I just tried to be myself and show love to everybody. Not in an in-your-face, happy-all-the-time way – just keeping it real so that I would influence my friends in love and in Christ. Sometimes I wasn't a great witness, but I think that I did make a positive impact on my peers by my actions.'

Though she was still finding her feet in high school, Katy's reputation was going before her within Goleta and its environs. And while it was a far cry from the Hollywood Bowl, her first paying gig came when she was invited to perform at the Santa Barbara Farmers' Market – just her, and the battered blue guitar she'd received as a thirteenth birthday present. 'This

was one way of making money as a young kid,' she told *Philstar*. 'It was fun because people would buy their fruit and vegetables, and there was a violinist in one corner, there's a kid doing some kind of drum interpretation, and then there was me at thirteen in my own little corner, singing my own silly songs. It was a great experience. It was great to be in front of people when you want to be in the music industry because it gives you a great read.'

Playing at the Farmers' Market not only gave Katy an easy means of making her own money, and a good musical grounding – or a 'great read' as she describes it – one of her appearances led to her getting her first break. For one of those watching her singing for her supper was Carol Thomas, a co-founder of the Christian organisation Action House, which was set up to help keep the homeless off the street while spreading the word of God. As luck would have it, Carol was in need of a promotions girl, and knew instantly that she'd found her girl.

Where she'd once accompanied her parents across America in their quest to spread the word of the Lord, on finding herself now doing the very same thing with Action House, Katy naturally became defensive about what she was doing. 'I think even as us in the Christian [music] industry, we should always be pushing the envelope, trying to be something a little bit better than the mainstream is!' she told *Christian Retailing*. 'We shouldn't be influenced by them; they should be influenced by us! The whole time we're influenced by them, we're so far behind that the average person's ear doesn't want to listen to it. I think we're worth more than that.'

'When I faced public high school, I didn't exclude myself from the worldly kids. I just tried to be myself and show love to everybody.' – Katy Perry

Yet, while Katy was protective of the Christian genre, she was – perhaps understandably, given her passion for music as a whole – becoming increasingly curious about that accursed rock'n'roll that was, in her parents' jaundiced eyes at least, polluting the minds of America's youth. But while Keith and Mary were keeping MTV and its evil music machinations away from their offspring's ears, for eight hours a day whilst Katy was at school they were helpless to prevent their daughter from being exposed to the latest news and gossip about the pop stars of the day. And sure enough, the day eventually dawned when her head was dramatically turned. 'I remember [the day] vividly,' she told *Star Pulse*. 'I was over at my friend's house and we were trying on all her clothes, and it was like a scene from a movie. She put on a CD, and it was "Killer Queen", and everything just flowed. We stopped dancing and sat on the edge of the bed listening to the lyrics of the song and thinking, "Oh, my Gosh!"

'It was a moment where everything kind of went in slow motion. The clouds moved away, the sun started shining and I was like, "I've found it! I've found an artist I want to be like!" Everybody has that one person they want to be, that poster on the wall – Elvis, Madonna. For me it was "Killer Queen" – I wanted to be like Freddie Mercury.'

It's easy to imagine her parents' reaction on discovering that the Almighty was in danger of being usurped in Katy's affections by the flamboyant Freddie, whose openly gay lifestyle had seen him succumb to AIDS in November 1991, but Katy had been seduced by his Bohemian Rhapsody. 'Freddie Mercury was a bad ass,' she told *BBC Entertainment*. 'It was kinda like he didn't care what anybody thought about him – he always brought the entertainment value to the show. Who would have thought that you would write a song about girls with big asses ["Fat Bottomed Girls"]? Everybody would sing along to it and, I don't know, he seemed like he had a good sense of humour in his life and was smart and intelligent, and, basically, said exactly what was on his mind – and I respect that. He never censored himself for the sake of anybody.'

The adult Katy would be even more direct in her appraisal of flamboyant Freddie: 'The music was totally different to anything I'd heard. I still love Freddie Mercury. He was flamboyant with a twist of the operatic. But more importantly, he just didn't give a f***.'

But of course, now that Pandora's music box had finally been opened, Katy was like the proverbial kid in the sweet shop, only instead of candy she had the *Billboard* 200's back catalogue to devour. 'I started little by little, asking, "Hey, you know, can I listen to the Beatles?"' she told *CBS News*. 'And I had friends that influenced their taste on me. You know, friends that I looked up to that were so much cooler – they knew about the world, you know? And I was just, "Wow, teach me everything."'

Her favourite female icon was Alanis Morissette – who, like the blaspheming Madge, would have no doubt caused consternation in the Hudson household for portraying God in the R-rated comedy *Dogma*, starring Matt Damon and Ben Affleck. Although it's fair to assume that at the time Katy – with her parents still serving as censors – would be oblivious to both the movie and its subject matter. 'The *Jagged Little Pill* record was a big influence on me,' she told *Star Pulse*. 'Everybody listened to that record and there was a song, if not all of them, that related to everyone. It was a soundtrack to life. I would listen to it for the summer over and over.'

Another 'forbidden fruit' that Katy was determined to pluck from the tree of life and take a juicy bite out of was dancing. 'I would go to the Santa Barbara Recreational Hall, and I would learn how to dance there,' she said. 'I was taught by some of the more seasoned dancers who were actually very involved in the scene. These girls would get out of their vintage Cadillacs with their pencil skirts and their tight little cardigans, and I thought it was so unique and different to what was going on in the 2000 or whatever the time zone was there . . . I was really attracted to having my own sense of style because I started swing-dancing, lindy hop and jitterbug.'

Though Katy was as fashion-conscious as the next teenager, and was keen to keep up with the trends of the day – her parents' guidelines allowing – it was seeing how the older dancers comported themselves while exuding a sexuality that wasn't to be found in any teen magazine that would lead to her reinventing her style. 'The forties have always been my biggest inspiration because I love the way the women held themselves,' she explained to *Black Book*. 'Everything was very manicured. Sure, they had pencil skirts on and big sweaters, but underneath that pencil skirt and that sweater, you know, that girl had a bullet bra, garter and stockings. She knew she was so sexy, and she didn't have to tell anybody, and that was, I think, so cool.'

But while the war-torn 1940s was undoubtedly her preferred era for femme fatale fashions, she was happy to take inspiration from more recent decades. 'I really like to look like a history book,' she later recalled. 'I can look 1940s, I can look 1970s hippie-chic, or sometimes I'll pull that '80s Brooklyn hip-hop kid with the door-knocker earrings.'

But that isn't to say that she didn't make the occasional fashion faux pas. 'I had the coolest fake leopard-print coat,' she told *The Guardian*. 'I went to school wearing this coat [but] everyone made fun of me. I sold it to the second-hand clothes shop two years later to get more clothes.'

*Katy attends a photo call before one of
her concerts in Berlin, Germany.*

3

Guilty Pleasures

'I think people appreciate a songwriter who shows different sides.
The whole angst thing is cool, but if that's all you've got, it's just
boring. Everything I write, whether it's happy or sad,
has a sense of humour to it.'

Having already succumbed to the temptations of rock'n'roll and jukebox jiving, it was only a matter of time before Katy dipped her toe into the third of her parents' unholy trinity – romance. But once again, her actions would have rocked Christian convention, as her first love wasn't a member of the opposite sex. 'When I fell in love for the first time,' she admitted, 'I didn't fall in love with a boy – her name was Anna! We shared everything, as best friends do. Anna was incredibly pretty, a sweet ballerina – she was perfect. Unfortunately, we never kissed each other – what a shame!'

While homosexuality – the love that dare not speak its name – is the ultimate taboo in America's so-called Bible Belt, lesbian crushes amongst teenage girls are far more prevalent than one might imagine. More often than not, these turn out to be experimentation rather than anything deeper, and though Katy would soon be revealing to the world, albeit tongue-in-cheek, that she'd kissed a girl (and liked it), her amorous attentions would soon enough turn to boys.

While she covertly listened to shameful secular music whenever the situation allowed, in public she continued to rock around the cross. 'I think a lot of people my age, we're looking for something real,' she told *Cross Rhythms*. 'I think everyone's tired of everyone slapping a bow on Christianity and saying, "This is actually about Jesus" – and they whisper it. They don't want any of that any more, they want somebody to step in their face and say, "Hey, what's up, don't be stupid – Jesus Christ is the only way."'

Katy was clearly going to need a vehicle to get God's message to those of her generation who were looking for 'something real', and fate once again provided a guiding hand when the demo tape that she'd recorded at the Dream Centre, a music-friendly Christian organisation based in Los Angeles, had its in-house producer David Henley in raptures. Though the tape was nothing more than an ad-hoc jamming session, Henley immediately recognised that Katy was destined for greatness. He was also astute enough to realise that while the songs on her demo were primarily aimed at the Christian market, she had the unique gift of crossover appeal.

*'The forties have always been my biggest inspiration because I love the way
the women held themselves,' Katy said of her 1940s fashion fetish.*

'When I fell in love for the first time, I didn't fall in love with a boy – her name was Anna! We shared everything, as best friends do.' – Katy Perry

It was through Henley's auspices that Katy's tape found its way to Dr Robert Pamplin Jr, who besides being the head of an evangelical church, was, more importantly – at least from Katy's perspective – also the head of the Christian music label Red Hill Records, both of which were based in Nashville, Tennessee. The timing couldn't have been more perfect had it been scripted, for Red Hill were on the lookout for a clean-cut female artist who might rival Christina Aguilera and Britney Spears in the pop stakes – whilst revealing a little less skin.

Yet while the dream of signing to a record company and releasing her songs to a mainstream audience was what inspired Katy to get up and sing, and while her parents readily approved of her going to Nashville to fulfil her ambitions, she was loath to leave her hometown. As she told *Christian Contemporary Music*: 'In Santa Barbara I'm five minutes from the beach, ten minutes from the mountains – I'm never moving to Nashville!'

But what might have appeared to be a show of childish petulance was actually her insecurities coming to the fore. For while she'd grown accustomed to singing in restaurants, at farmers' markets or for church gatherings, the thought of recording an album for real in Nashville – the home of country music – simply overwhelmed her.

Of course, once Katy arrived in Nashville, any self-doubt she might have had quickly

Left and above: There's no such thing as too much pink: Katy performs onstage at Spike TV's Second Annual Guys Choice Awards in Culver City, California.

 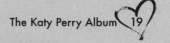

evaporated into the ether. 'So I'd go to Nashville and I'd be around all these veteran music writers, and they would show me how to carve a song,' she later recounted. 'I saw how important that was and it just gave me a format. You need to have an arch in the middle [of each song]. You have to have your verse, chorus, verse, chorus, bridge and then chorus. I didn't know that – it can be so many different ways, and you don't even have to have rules to writing a song.'

Though her dreams were coming true, her relocating to Nashville to record her debut album meant she had to wave goodbye to high school in favour of enrolling herself on an internet home-schooling programme. 'I really wish I could go [back] to high school,' she lamented to *Christian Retailing*. 'I went there for a semester and I loved it. [But] you have to sacrifice some things. Everyone's thinking, "Oh, she has to sacrifice working and school – pity, pity, pity! I'm going to cry a river for you!" It's just that I always want to keep my brain on and keep learning.'

It is also worth remembering that at this juncture Katy had only just turned sixteen, and though everyone was going out of their way to facilitate her arrival in Nashville, she still felt like the new kid in the playground. 'It seemed like everybody knew everybody else, and I didn't know anyone,' she told *Christian Music Central*. 'It made me feel like the new kid all over again, just like growing up. I would even feel intimidated about playing the five chords I know pretty well.'

'I don't want to put on some kind of front that everything is good when it's not. I wanted to keep it real, but still give people hope.' – Katy Perry

Red Hill had, of course, anticipated Katy's anxieties and assigned her to songwriter Brian White, who, aside from helping Katy with song ideas, was also on hand to mentor her through each and every step of the recording process. While recording an album was serious work, he went out of his way to make the experience as pleasurable as possible.

It was also White's task to ensure that Katy's songs could be assimilated not only by teenagers, but by Christians of all ages. He – like everyone at the label – recognised that in order to ensure the record was the success they were all hoping it would be, Katy would have to be skilfully guided away from the traditional Christian contemporary sound that had served her up to his point, in order to attract a more modern audience. And it hadn't gone unnoticed that there were too many cooks in Katy's kitchen; she was getting advice from all corners, and as a result was desperately trying to please everyone.

Katy herself would admit as much to *Christian Retailing*: 'Too many influences on you, you don't know what to do,' she said. 'Everyone was like, "Be that way," and I was like, "God, just help me to know what I want to be!" Sure, you can always sit and listen to what people have to say, but most of it's bad for your ear.'

Had Katy's album been a compilation of traditional gospel songs or hymns, then Red Hill would surely have been onto a winner. But faith is like a Rorschach test, in that while each and every Christian recognises the one true God, they do so from their own individual perspective. And while Katy's odes to the Lord would appeal to Christians of her own age, more seasoned listeners were left somewhat confused. For while tracks such as 'Trust In Me', and 'Growing Pains' are pretty self-explanatory, as Katy is obviously asking those around her to give her the time and space to find herself, 'When There's Nothing Left' – in which she describes a

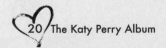

romantic relationship between herself and her creator – is bordering on blasphemy.

While Katy considered her singing talent to be a gift from God, and was far too humble to ever consider herself as being better than anyone else, she was worried about what reaction to expect following the album's release. 'I was struggling with the fact that I would have the huge responsibility of how others would be affected through what I was saying or doing on stage,' she admitted on her website. 'I don't want to put on some kind of front that everything is good when it's not. I wanted to keep it real, but still give people hope. I was trying to figure out how to combine the two, so I put my gifts on the shelf for a period of time.

'I looked back and realised that God was with me through this season of my life. He knew one day I would wake up and remember the amazing gift I was given and how so many other people would love to be on the stage that I had been letting collect dust.'

Once the album was finished, instead of catching the first flight back to Santa Barbara, Katy decided to remain in Nashville and moved in with her Red Hill assigned publicist, the aptly-named Mandy Collinger-Parsons. Alabaster Arts – the management company recently set up by Christian folk singer Jennifer Knapp and her business partner Steven Thomas – stepped in to sign Katy after seeing her make one of her casual in-store promotional performances.

Katy made her Nashville debut at the Douglas Corner Café a few weeks later. But the transformation from cutesy, girl-next-door Katy Hudson to the sassy Katy Perry we

Mom's the word: Katy and her mother, Mary Hudson, at the launch party for her album, One Of The Boys, *in Los Angeles.*

know and love today was still in the future, and she took to the café's stage dressed in jeans and T-shirt, and with little or no make-up. Indeed, those in attendance could have been forgiven for thinking someone had made a mistake in putting this doe-eyed school kid on the same bill as seasoned veterans. But their amused indifference disappeared the moment she opened her mouth to sing.

Faith Won't Fail

*'I know sometimes if I don't think about what I do,
or think about the things I say, then I'll ruin it for everybody,
and keep giving that stereotype of teens – that they're irresponsible,
and not doing anything with their lives.'*

In February 2001, Katy embarked on a nationwide tour with Christian music acts V*Enna, Earthsuit and Phil Joel, but while her music was perfectly suited to the places they'd be playing, her quirky personality and seemingly limitless youthful exuberance – both on and off stage – was a little unsettling for those in authority.

While the disapproving adults in the audience would wag a finger or tut-tut at Katy's antics, people her own age welcomed her with open arms. She was a sixteen-year-old girl who was still finding her way, and desperate to be accepted by her fellow Christians. In penning her own songs she was not just revealing her innermost feelings, but also baring her soul to her audience. 'I started writing songs when I realised that singing other people's lyrics was more an expression of their heart than mine,' she told *Christian Music Central*. 'Writing this album was very important to me. I felt I'd been given a message and was supposed to voice it in my own words. I want to be an artist, not just someone who puts her voice on a CD – and I didn't want to be written off as just another teenager with a record deal.'

While Katy had been out on the road, Mandy Collinger-Parsons had been busy sending out sample singles featuring 'Search Me' and 'Last Call' to drum up attention for the parent album – featuring a close-up of an innocent-looking Katy on the cover – which was released in March 2001.

The initial reviews were praiseworthy indeed, with *Christianity Today* complimenting her songwriting talents, and comparing Katy's throaty and soulful vocals to those of Fiona Apple and Sarah McLachlan. The review ended by hinting that if the debut album was anything to go by then the world could expect to be hearing the name Katy Hudson more and more in the coming months.

However, this good news was quickly followed by some bad when Red Hill announced that, due to financial issues, it would have to drop some acts from its roster. 'They told me

*Katy performs at the Victoria's Secret fashion show in New York, wearing
an eye-catching purple number from designer Todd Thomas.*

some of the female artists were going on the chopping block,' she told Effect Radio. 'I was only seventeen, and I was devastated. I prayed, which I didn't do that much . . . then I got an invitation to sing at Dr Pamplin's church because someone had given him my album, and reminded him I already worked for him. I guess you would call it a miracle – but I say it's just God looking after his own.'

Despite Katy having Dr Pamplin Jr's support, Red Hill's financial problems meant that only a certain amount of cash could be set aside for promoting and marketing her debut album. And while those that managed to get hold of a copy were making appreciative noises, the overwhelming majority of America's Christians remained blithely ignorant of its existence. But any hope that this glaring oversight might soon be rectified withered on the bough when Red Hill Records announced it was going into liquidation.

It was only following the label's collapse that Katy was made aware of just how limited Red Hill's distribution network actually was, for her album had sold just 200 copies.

While Katy might well have chosen to remain on her righteous path had Red Hill Records survived, on finding herself standing at a crossroads she decided to pull up a stool and consider her options. And with her faith beginning to falter, there really was only one option.

'I started writing songs when I realised that singing other people's lyrics was more an expression of their heart than mine.' – Katy Perry

Katy returned to Santa Barbara and set about recording some new demos. The only drawback being that whereas most teenagers contemplating a musical career have been weaned on pop music, and can cite endless influences to guide the producer's hand, Katy was completely in the dark. Up until then her knowledge of mainstream music was extremely limited. And sneakily listening to borrowed CDs through headphones under the covers whilst her parents were asleep didn't allow for scrutinising production techniques. 'Growing up, I wasn't really allowed to listen to a whole lot of what my mom would call secular music so I didn't have a whole lot of references,' she admitted to *The Star Scoop*. 'When the producer I was doing my demos with was like, "Okay, so who would you want to work with if you could work with anybody?" I was like, "I really have no idea."'

But again, it seemed as though fate was guiding her hand, for on returning to her hotel she switched onto the hitherto forbidden VH1, which just so happened to be screening an interview with six-time Grammy Award-winning producer Glen Ballard. Ballard, whose first production credit was on Michael Jackson's squillion-selling *Thriller*, was talking about his work on Alanis Morissette's sixteen-time platinum-selling album, *Jagged Little Pill*.

One can only imagine what her producer's reaction was on hearing that Katy – whose debut album hadn't accrued enough royalties for a Hershey bar – wanted to work with the hottest producer on the planet. Thankfully, however, he believed in her enough to pull the requisite strings to gain Katy an audition with Ballard. But as Katy herself subsequently admitted to *The Star Scoop*, even she didn't expect anything to come of the meeting. Indeed, she was so convinced that she was on a wasted errand that she told her dad, who drove her to the audition, to leave the engine running. 'I said, "Dad, stay in the car,"' she told the online

The butterfly effect: Katy on the red carpet at the 2008 MTV Video Music Awards in Los Angeles.

magazine. 'I'm just gonna go in, play a song for this guy and come back out. And I guess it went well, because I got the call the next day.'

Ballard invited her to relocate to Los Angeles with a promise to help make all her dreams come true. Katy was thrilled at the chance to work with Ballard and readily accepted. Somewhat surprisingly, given that Los Angeles was a den of heathen iniquity, and that Katy was still a minor, her parents were equally enthusiastic and gave their blessing – but only on the proviso that she finish her schooling first.

Though she was desperate to develop her Do-Re-Mis instead of learning her ABCs, Katy did as her parents asked and returned to high school. Such was her determination to link up with Ballard that she gained her GED (General Educational Diploma) within her first freshman year. Now that she had the necessary qualification should her dream fail to materialise, she set about cramming her possessions into bags. Before bidding a fond farewell to her former life, however, she attended the Dos Pueblos Homecoming Ball. 'I went to Homecoming with a senior,' she told MTV. 'That made me feel really cool, because when you catch a senior for homecoming or for prom, or whatever it is, you've made it.'

'Once I stopped being chaperoned and realised I had a choice in life, I was like, "Wow, there are a lot of choices."' – Katy Perry

She made the ninety-five-mile journey from Santa Barbara to Los Angeles in the brand-new car she'd treated herself to, and each and every mile of the way she would have been imagining what awaited her in the big bad city. 'The things that I thought when I was fifteen or sixteen didn't make sense just because my perspective had changed. I'd seen more of the world,' she told *The Scotsman*. 'I'd lived more of life and met more different types of people. When I started out in my gospel music, my perspective then was a bit enclosed and very strict and everything I had in my life at that time was church-related. I didn't know there was another world that existed beyond that. So when I left home and saw all of that, it was like, "Ohmigosh, I fell down the rabbit hole and there's this whole Alice in Wonderland right there!"'

It was whilst she was navigating her way along the rabbit-hole that she encountered her first serious boyfriend Matt Thiessen, Canadian-born frontman of Christian rockers Relient K, whom she'd first encountered on the Christian touring circuit. And while Thiessen was still deeply committed to serving God, he was more than happy to allow beer onto the menu when the couple embarked on their nightly Mad-Hatter's Tea Parties, and it was perhaps inevitable that Katy would break her longstanding promise to God. 'My boyfriend [Thiessen] and I went a little too far, and I felt I'd fallen so far away from God,' she told *Seventeen*. 'I doubted myself and my strength. I was so weak at the time in my relationship with Christ.'

Of course, now that she'd given up her chastity, she began to question some of the other taboos that had thus far governed her outlook on life. 'Letting go [of my religion] was just a process,' she told *Christianity Today*. 'Meeting gay people or Jewish people, and realising they were fine was a big part of it. Once I stopped being chaperoned and realised I had a choice in life, I was like, "Wow, there are a lot of choices." I began to become a sponge for all that I had missed . . . I was as curious as the [proverbial] cat. But I'm not dead yet.'

Let them eat cake: Katy shows off a Neiman Marcus-designed purse at the MTV Europe Music Awards in Liverpool.

 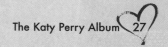

5

Rock Goddess

'When I first started at seventeen in Los Angeles, the hit song was "Complicated", and everyone wanted me to write a "Complicated". I'm like, "Look, that's Avril, this is me."'

In 2003, it seemed as though all her hard work had paid off when Island Def Jam signed her up. But with Katy having only recently crossed the divide from gospel to pop, the renowned hip-hop label was unsure how to best promote her new material. Like Ballard, Def Jam had been on the lookout for a feisty, girl singer to compete with Britney Spears and Christina Aguilera, whose debut albums – *Baby One More Time* and *Christina Aguilera* – had both scored a Number One hit on the *Billboard* Hot 100. And though the label bosses recognised Katy's potential, they were doubtful that she had the sassy attitude to convince the kids she was the real deal and swiftly dropped her from their roster of acts.

Having Glen Ballard fighting her corner meant Katy was always going to have a distinct advantage over the competition, but when Columbia came a-calling with a contract, the label did so with a set of cast-iron stipulations. For whilst Columbia's powers-that-be were as keen as Island Def Jam had been to add a sassy pop princess to their roster, they treated the process of finding their artists as though it were a car assembly production line, and signed up several girls with a view to turning one of them into that year's model. Though Katy got as far as recording an album's worth of material for Columbia, she was one of those told that instead of making pop records she could 'go back to Middle America and pop out babies' instead. Her album was indefinitely shelved.

As Columbia had been more appreciative of Katy's talents than Island Def Jam, their eleventh-hour decision to pass on the album must have been infinitely more painful. However, rather than see her crawl back into her shell, the rejection simply spurred her on. And while she continued knocking at record-company doors in the hope that one of them would go one step further than Columbia, she also perused the classifieds in the trade music papers. One ad that particularly caught her eye was from The Matrix, the three-piece songwriting and production team – Lauren Christy, Graham Edwards and Scott Spock – who were renowned both for taking failed artists

Rock'n'roll queen: Katy onstage at Paper *magazine's 'Beautiful People' party at the Maritime Hotel in New York.*

'It turned into a situation where for years I was telling my friends that I was going to have a record out – like I had the CD art and everything, and then it wouldn't happen.' – Katy Perry

and turning them into platinum-selling stars, and for re-energising the careers of household names such as Ricky Martin and David Bowie. The talented trio had also provided hit singles for the likes of Christina Aguilera, Britney Spears, Shakira, Busted, and nu-metalheads Korn.

It seemed The Matrix had been approached by Sony Records to come out from the shadows where they preferred to work, and develop a Fleetwood Mac-esque band which would be fronted by young, good-looking male and female singers. Unknown British singer Adam Longlands was selected for the as-yet-unnamed band's male lead, while Katy – having been given a glowing reference by Columbia – clinched the female lead.

The trio, recognising that Katy was more than just a pretty face, were willing to listen to her ideas for songs. They also revolutionised Katy's way of thinking in terms of recording, and taught her 21st-century production techniques. Up until then, Katy confessed that her approach to music had been positively prehistoric: 'I have a four-track in the trunk of my car that I take everywhere,' she told *INK19* magazine. 'Everybody's taking about gadgets and stuff like that and getting all technical and I'm like, "Yeah, I've got a four-track that my ex-boyfriend gave me as a going-away gift that I write all my songs on."'

The finished album consisted of ten tracks, three of which were Katy solos, and five duets with co-singer Adam Longlands. One of these was 'Broken', which The Matrix had earmarked for the first single. What the trio had failed to mention to either Adam or Katy during the recording

Above and right: *Katy performs her breakthrough single 'I Kissed A Girl' at the 51st Annual Grammy Awards.*

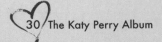

process, however, was that the song – under the title 'What Do You Do?' – had bombed when it was released the previous year by another of their acts, The Troys. And this startling omission was the snowball that became an avalanche of mistrust between protégés and producers; so much so, that within weeks of its release date The Matrix decided to shelve the album indefinitely.

No one could have blamed Katy if she'd turned her back on music after this latest setback, but she had faith in what she was doing. In August 2005, Columbia Records – no doubt having monitored Katy's progress with The Matrix – had decided to release six of the tracks she'd previously recorded for them as a limited edition album in Japan. And, so as not to see herself confused with actress Kate Hudson, Katy adopted her mother's maiden name 'Perry'. To promote the mini-album Katy recorded a promotional DVD which contained video clips of all six songs.

But once again the light emanating from the end of the tunnel would prove to be a tantalising chimera, as in early 2006 Columbia announced they were cancelling her contract. Though Glen Ballard still believed she had the talent to make it, and urged her to treat this latest disappointment as merely a temporary setback, Katy was beginning to think she was being punished for daring to sing secular songs rather than homages to her God. And with her stuttering career once again on hold, for the first time since setting out on her journey, she contemplated packing it all in.

'I had already been through being on a big label and them telling me, "You're going to have a record out," and then finally there would be complete silence.' – Katy Perry

Returning to Santa Barbara with her tail between her legs, however, was never an option, as Katy would have rather died than suffer the whispered 'I told you so's on entering the room. 'It turned into a situation where for years I was telling my friends that I was going to have a record out – like I had the CD art and everything, and then it wouldn't happen,' she later recalled. 'I was pretty much a joke.'

So instead of going home – and to the consternation of those who did care what Katy did next – she fell into LA's party scene with wild abandon, intent on drinking and dancing her woes away. 'My music wasn't happening,' she subsequently confessed to *Christian Music Central*. 'I just felt kind of slow in everything, and my relationship with God slowed down.' To the casual observer it would have looked as though 'carefree Katy' was having a rare old time as she drank and danced till dawn, but inside she was hurting. And it wasn't only her pride that had taken a beating, as her reckless lifestyle was also impacting on her bank balance. Having suffered the indignity of having to repay Columbia's advance, she also faced the mortification of having her car – the symbol of her supposed success – repossessed. Glen Ballard did what he could to help by getting her occasional bits of work, but while cameo appearances in promo videos put food on the table for a time, they were never going to pay the rent. And the final humiliation came when her cheques began to bounce. 'I'd write cheques, and in the memo section, I'd write "Please God!"' she joked to *E! Entertainment*. 'My Rolodex was filled with numbers to the brim, so why isn't this happening? I said to myself, "If I don't make it by twenty-five, I'm gonna refocus."'

'I came close to quitting when I couldn't pay my bills,' she told *Star Pulse*. 'When I had already been through being on a big label and them telling me, "You're going to have a

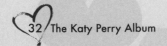

record out," and then finally there would be complete silence. That ultimately meant that it wasn't happening after all the hard work that I'd put into it. It's like completing your debut movie and it never being able to come out, it's all you've worked on in life.'

But as the weeks continued to roll by without any sign of a reverse in her misfortunes, Katy was forced to face the reality of her situation: if she wanted to remain in LA to pursue her dreams, she would have to take a nine-to-five job. Thankfully, getting a job in LA is much easier than getting a break, and she found a position with Taxi Music, an independent A&R (Artist and Repertoire) company which not only aimed to set aspiring musicians up with publishers and record labels, but also gave impartial advice on how to maximise their chances. Ironically, given that Katy considered herself a failure, her job was to critique and mentor those who'd suffered similar disappointments.

'That was the most depressing moment of my hustle,' she told *The Guardian*. 'I was sitting there in a cubicle with twenty-five other trying-to-make-it failed artists in a box listening to the worst music you've ever heard in your entire life. Having no money, writing bad cheques, renting a car after two cars had been repossessed, trying to give people constructive criticism and hope,

Katy showcases her guitar skills on a white Gibson Les Paul, onstage in Pontiac, Michigan.

when all I really wanted was to jump out of the building or cut my ears off and say, "I can't help you! I can't catch a break. What am I gonna say to you? And you sing out of tune."'

While it's a well-worn cliché, once you reach rock-bottom the only way you can go is up, but try as she might it seemed as though the angels had abandoned Katy to her fate. For whilst doling out platitudes and career advice to her fellow failures, she continued writing songs and sending demo tapes off in the hope that someone would rescue her from her nightmare. For a heartbeat it seemed as though her prayers had been answered when Capitol Records – who would subsequently sign Katy – expressed interest before then refusing to take further calls. 'I had someone say to me, "Psst, you should probably go home because you're never gonna get signed again. You're pretty much damaged goods, and you should be in the defect aisle [the bargain bins in supermarkets],"' she told *Entertainment Weekly*. 'And I'm twenty at this point. I'm like, "I'm defective goods already?"'

6

Californian Gurl

'It's not a negative connotation ["Ur So Gay"]. It's not "you're so gay", like "you're so lame", but the fact of the matter is that this boy should've been gay. I was talking ex-boyfriends.'

Rather than listen to or lash out at her detractors – especially those snidely saying she was intent on being famous simply for fame's sake, Katy channelled her frustrations into writing and recording new songs with Glen Ballard. But while she could have been forgiven for thinking the world was against her, unbeknownst to her she did have supporters in high places. One of these was Angelica Cob-Bachler, a senior publicist at Columbia Records, who'd questioned the label's decision to drop Katy. Indeed, such was Angelica's enthusiasm for Katy's hitherto neglected talents that she told anyone willing to listen that it wouldn't be long before the world knew her name. And when she left Columbia in the spring of 2006 to take up a similar role at Capitol Records, one of the first things she did was to tell her new co-workers of Columbia's mistake in letting Katy go.

Though Chris Anokute, who worked within Capitol's A&R department, readily admitted to having never even heard of Katy, they respected Angelica's knowledge enough to agree to listen to a three-track demo tape which she happened to have in her possession. The three songs on the tape were 'Simple', which had appeared on Columbia's Japan-only album released the previous year, and two new songs: 'Thinking Of You' and 'Waking Up In Vegas' – both of which would ultimately feature on *One Of The Boys*.

On hearing the tape, and recognising Katy's ability to pen upbeat singalongs and tear-jerking ballads with seemingly consummate ease, Chris Anokute found himself in complete agreement with Angelica's appraisal. 'I thought, "This is a Number One record,"' he told *Hit Quarters*. 'I took the demo and went to Jason Flom's office (Flom being Capitol's CEO at the time), and said, "Oh, my God, I've found the next Avril Lavigne meets Alanis Morissette!"' On hearing the tape, however, Flom remained unimpressed. Unlike Anokute, he had heard of Katy, and also knew Columbia hadn't been the first label to let Katy go. He was, however, impressed by Anokute's enthusiasm and agreed to accompany him to see Katy perform live when the opportunity next presented itself. 'Because I was so passionate about it, Jason decided to come to a showcase,' Anokute said.

What's in a name? Katy belts it out onstage at the V Festival in Chelmsford, England.

The two caught Katy's show at The Viper Room, and while Flom was impressed enough to go and see a second performance at the Polo Lounge, he left still feeling unsure of whether Katy was worth the time and expenditure. And that would normally have been the end of it had Anokute not persisted with his one-man crusade: 'I [was] so passionate about it that every single week I'm beating him up, trying to convince him to sign her, saying, "Jason, we'll find the record, we'll develop her, we'll figure it out! There is something special about her – I know she is a star. Who cares if she was dropped?"' he told *Hit Quarters*. 'We were determined to get this deal through . . . Almost seven weeks later, Jason emails me: "It's great. What are we waiting for? Let's sign the girl."'

What exactly had caused this eventual turnaround in Flom's thinking Anokute doesn't say, but it seems Katy's road to Damascus passed by the Capitol Records Building on Hollywood and Vine. Needless to say, she didn't care what Flom's reasons were, but Anokute's call – which came whilst she was gently letting down yet another failed performer at Taxi's offices, was sweet music to her ears. 'I got a phone call from the guy that ran Capitol Records because they were going to sign me, and then decided not to sign me. That was my third record label to do that to me,' she told *Seventeen*. 'I was like, "I'm not going through this again!" and he called me a few months later when I was sitting in that cubicle, and said, "I'm sorry, I almost made the biggest mistake of my life in not signing you. I really believe in you! Let's just do it, let's just try!" I was like, "Really?" and he was like, "Yeah, let's just try!" So we did it.'

'I'm not trying to hide anything, I'm trying to sell records. I've always wanted to do a big pop record, and that's what I'm starting with.' – Katy Perry

Since arriving in LA at the turn of the millennium Katy had penned some seventy songs. And whilst the majority were flowery, soft-hearted ditties about teenage love and angst, and didn't quite fit in with the image Capitol had decided on for her, there was enough harder-edged, newer material within Katy's canon to form the basis of an album. Katy believed she'd honed her craft to a point where she could now critique artists in the charts, and not just those trudging a forlorn path to Taxi Music's door. 'I get pissed off when singers don't take advantage of a good melody and a beat, and put some kind of lyrics that make people feel something,' she told *The Daily Telegraph*. 'It doesn't matter if it makes them want to dance or laugh or cry, or raises the hairs on their arms.'

But while she was undoubtedly grateful for Capitol's showing faith in her pop potential, she let it be known that the man upstairs still featured in her game plan. 'Yeah, you may have signed me to be a Christina Aguilera, but I'm doing this for me and God,' she told *Christian Music Central*. 'I'm doing this because it's my time now. I didn't do this because you had some kind of idea that I would be somebody I'm not.'

Yet she soon clouded the holy water, first of all by insisting to *Black Book* magazine that she was 'all about mainstream music'. 'I'm not trying to hide anything, I'm trying to sell records,' she added defiantly. 'I've always wanted to do a big pop record, and that's what I'm starting with.' And any remaining doubt about her new career path was soon dispelled: 'I'm completely shameless!' she told *Music OMH*. 'I love pop music. I've been around kids that hate selling records and enjoy being the starving artist. But I want to play stadiums. I want to sell records. I want to be a pop girl!'

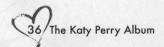

Shady lady: Katy arrives at the Mercedes-Benz Fashion Week in New York.

When she'd first signed to Red Hill, the then sixteen-year-old Katy had declared to the world that she was who she was, and that she wasn't going to let anybody change her. But of course, six years of struggle had brought about a radical change to her perceptions, and she was more than happy to rock'n'roll away the gospel music millstone that had been hanging around her neck. When *CBS News* subsequently asked her what the innocent sixteen-year-old Katy Hudson might have said had she glimpsed her future sexy, pop pin-up self, she was at least honest enough to admit that the idea had always been lurking at the back of her mind.

'Ultimately,' she confided in *Star Scoop*, 'I sold my soul to the devil.'

Since Salvation Army founder William Booth was credited with questioning why it was that the devil had all the best tunes, every tunesmith this side of the River Styx has strived to compete with 'Old Nick'. But although Katy's debut Capitol single 'Ur So Gay', which was offered as a free download when released on Tuesday, 20 November 2007, brought her no airplay, it did elicit plenty of media exposure owing to the song's supposed 'gay-baiting' title. That the subsequent CD single was issued with a 'parental advisory explicit content' sticker showed just how far Katy's halo had slipped since her gospel days.

Katy would later explain to *Prefix* that the single was only meant as a 'soft hello', rather than a big single, or even to show what the parent album would be about. She also told the magazine that she'd initially contemplated covering a Queen song for her debut release in tribute to her hero Freddie Mercury: 'There were a couple of choices in the pile for covers. I actually wanted to do a Queen cover, but there wasn't anything they would play in the club. So I'm back to square one, and I go out dancing with my girls. "Use Your Love", the original version by the Outfield, comes on, and immediately every girl hits the dance floor. Everybody's out there dancing and trying to hit these notes. It was the best time, and I wanted to capture that on "Ur So Gay".'

While the single failed to trouble the *Billboard* Hot 100, Katy was still forced into publicly defending its lyrics. 'It's about those guys that wear the guy-liner, and use the flat irons and wear my jeans – I want to wear my jeans!' she told the lesbian magazine, *Diva*. 'It's about guys who spend more time in the mirror than their girlfriends do – and I wrote it after being dumped. It was one of those relationships where the dumpage lasts longer than the usual relationship, unfortunately, and I just remember after, finally, it was the last straw, kicking me out of the apartment and not coming back. I went back to my house and I was a little upset.'

'"Ur So Gay" is about guys who spend more time in the mirror than their girlfriends do – and I wrote it after being dumped.' – Katy Perry

And with a little help from her roommate Katy channelled her upset into song. 'I had this verse that I had been developing in my head and I played it to her and I was like, "I don't know what to say in the chorus, he's just. Like, so gay," and she's like, "Say that." I'm like, "Okay, I'll say that!" It's taking the piss out of that emo scene.'

'It's any guy who wears eye-liner and smudges it,' she added for *Buzznet*. 'It's just taking the piss out of this scene we call emo. There's a little emo in all of us.'

'Every time I play that song, everybody has come back laughing,' she told *Prefix*. 'I'm not the type of person who walks around calling everything gay. That song is about a specific guy that I used to date and specific issues that he had. The song is about my ex wearing guy-liner and taking emo pictures of himself in the bathroom mirror. The listeners have to read the context of the song and decide for themselves.'

'The fact of the matter is that we live in a metrosexual world,' she told *The Times* when the conservative British broadsheet questioned her motives. 'You know a girl might walk into a bar, meet a boy and discover he's more manicured than she is, and they can't figure it out. Is he wearing foundation and a bit of bronzer? But he's buying me drinks at the same time . . . I'm not saying, "You're so gay, you're so lame." I'm saying, "You're so gay, but I don't understand it because you don't like boys!"'

Katy was so proud of her work that she showed it to the guy in question: 'We had a conversation about it,' she told *Metro Mix*. 'We had some words. He was fine. I played him the song and said, "C'mon, motherf**ker, you're gonna dump me?" and he was like, "Oh, s**t."'

And of course, if Katy thought her first single was courting controversy, it was but a storm in a teacup when compared to the furore that would surround her next effort.

G'day, mate: Katy finds plenty to smile about during a promotional trip to Melbourne, Australia.

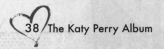

7

Some Girls Do . . .

'It was a huge moment for me. I broke out in hives.
Yeah, I'm like, "Madonna doesn't have time to listen to music, let
alone know my first and last name, let alone be my cheerleader!"
Yeah, my dreams were definitely coming true.'

Though Jason Flom and Capitol's other suits were happy that 'Ur So Gay' had lifted Katy out of her personal purgatory and into the public conscience, they were ultimately looking for a quick return on their investment. So rather than allow Katy sole songwriting duties on the follow-up single, they decided to hedge their bets by assembling a formidable songwriting/ production team, which included Max Martin, who'd written Britney Spears's career-launching 1999 chart smash '. . . Baby One More Time', and Cathy Dennis, who was responsible for penning Kylie Minogue's 2001 worldwide hit and perennial club classic 'Can't Get You Out Of My Head'.

Yet, despite the array of songwriting talent Capitol had assembled, it was Katy who provided the inspiration for the song that would launch her career. '"I Kissed A Girl" was born as an idea in my head,' she subsequently revealed to *BBC News*. 'The chorus actually popped into my head when I woke up. It was one of those moments where you hear artists talking about songs they got in their dreams, or in the middle of the night.'

But whilst she couldn't bring herself to reveal the song's semi-autobiographical subject matter to the stiff-collared BBC, she felt more relaxed speaking about her unrequited childhood love to *Diva* magazine's predominantly lesbian circulation. 'I was obsessed with her,' she confessed. 'I did everything she did. I couldn't believe that one person could be so delicate and flower-like and beautiful. She didn't even have to work at it. She'd wake up in the morning and she's just like a fawn; a little Bambi. She was always in the back of my head as that iconic beauty.'

'Everyone takes the song and relates it to their situation, they can see it however they want to see it,' she later opined. 'Love it; hate it, for me it was about us girls. When we're young, we're very touchy-feely. We have slumber party singalongs; we make up dance routines in our pyjamas. We're a lot more intimate in a friendship than guys can be. It's not perverse but just sweet, that's what the song is about.'

Yet Katy was quick to insist that she herself was neither gay nor bisexual – even if 'I Kissed A Girl' was in part inspired by her feelings for actress Scarlett Johansson – and that she was very

*Lipstick and leopard-print: Katy promotes her Australian
tour in Sydney's Intercontinental Hotel.*

All I want for Christmas: Katy performs at KIIS FM's Jingle Ball in Anaheim, California.

much in love with her new boyfriend, the rapper Travie McCoy. Still, the song inevitably enraged gay rights activists everywhere over its blatant, sexually exploitative lyrics.

If Chris Anokute is to be believed, the song, which to date has sold in excess of six million copies worldwide, might not have got beyond the recording studio door. 'When she [Katy] was cutting "I Kissed A Girl", she comes into my office and plays me the song on her guitar,' he recalled for *Hit Quarters*. 'I thought, "Oh, my God, if the music is incredible, then this is a career record." I couldn't wait to start playing it to people in the office, but for some reason people weren't getting it. One [unnamed] influential senior exec told me it sounded like an international club track. Other people said, "This is never going to get played on the radio. How can we sell this? How's this going to be played in the Bible Belt?"'

But Anokute's gut-feeling told him they were onto a winner: 'I was twenty-four. I know what young people out there listen to,' he added. 'I've partied and hung out socially with Katy and her friends, and I know how she responded to music, so I kept on fighting. I convinced one of the radio guys to believe in the record. Dennis Reese [Capitol's Senior Vice-President of Promotions] saw the vision. So I had to use him to try to convince everyone to give this record a shot. So we have one shot. If this doesn't go, Katy is probably going to get dropped. We have to make a statement.'

Yet if Katy is to be believed, she wasn't prepared to make said statement: 'When the label wanted to go with "I Kissed A Girl", I was like, "Nooo!"' she insisted to *Entertainment Weekly*. '"I'm gonna come off like that's the only subject I know how to sing about!"'

Of course, Katy soon came around to Capitol's way of thinking, and she'd been writing songs long enough to know that if she couldn't stop humming the tune to 'I Kissed A Girl' to herself every hour of the day then the record – if it was marketed right – was going to be big. 'I knew this song was going to be the song that could possibly open all the doors,' she told *E! Entertainment*. 'I knew it was just the kick-off.'

Yet while the accompanying promotional video – directed by Kinga Burza – features a provocatively-clad Katy gyrating to the music with a bevy of burlesque beauties set against a Moulin Rouge backdrop, there is not even a hint of same-sex kissing. Indeed, the only thing to get a cuddle from Katy during the whole shoot was her cat, the punningly-named Kitty Purry.

While Katy and everyone at Capitol knew that in a perfect world they had a monster hit on their hands, there were a couple of flies in Katy's otherwise delicious soup. One was that with 'I Kissed A Girl' following on the back of 'Ur So Gay', Katy – albeit owing to Capitol's decision to release the song as the follow-up single – was setting herself up for one almighty backlash at the hands of the gay community. The second and more important issue – at least as far as Capitol, and indeed, Katy's career were concerned – was whether the country's radio stations would deem the song suitable for their respective play-lists.

Capitol's fears, however, evaporated into the ether when The River, a radio station based in the devoutly religious Nashville, became the first station to add 'I Kissed A Girl' to their play-list. And whilst the station's CEO, Rich Davis, did get a few calls from irate mothers threatening to switch stations if they played the song again, the anticipated gay community backlash failed to materialise. Indeed, the majority of The River's listeners headed for their local record shop.

Of course, the irony of it all was that Katy was subsequently criticised for not actually kissing one of the other girls in the 'I Kissed A Girl' video. Though such a ridiculous

Belle of the ball: Katy onstage at the Q102 Jingle Ball in Camden, New Jersey.

criticism wasn't worthy of a response, Katy felt compelled to explain herself. 'I didn't want to be so literal,' she told *Diva*. 'This isn't your freak show of girls making out. Some people still have a problem with it, but there's much more crazy, raunchy stuff on MTV – I mean, have you ever seen a hip-hop video? My perspective is a little bit tongue-in-cheek, cute, flirtatious, [and] curious. A little Betty Boop here and there . . . It walks a line of provocative. But I've seen people f**king hop off the line and jump in the pool!'

While Katy was not without her detractors in the gay community – as well as those within the music industry – what they all should have realised was that 'I Kissed A Girl' wasn't demeaning lesbianism, it was simply Katy revealing that she knew what it was like to live in a prejudicial environment, and what her parents' reaction would have been had she confessed to having feelings for another girl. 'I understand where people who experience prejudice are coming from – I've grown up around a lot of ignorance,' she told *Diva*.

She went one confessional step further during an interview with *The Advocate*. 'I guess

it's a subject that is close to my heart,' she told the magazine. 'I have a lot of friends who are gay, and I have kissed a girl. I grew up in a very strict environment where that was considered what you call an abomination – and I f**king hate that word!'

Katy's admission that she'd kissed a girl – which under the Constitution gave her the automatic right to sing about it should she chose – should have been sufficient to put the matter to rest. Yet she still found herself under attack. She was also forced to defend herself against accusations that writing 'I Kissed A Girl' was nothing more than a crass marketing ploy to cash in on male adolescent fantasies. 'Some people are fascinated with the idea of a great storyline: good girl, Christian parents, goes bad,' she told Q magazine. '"I Kissed A Girl" provided the perfect storyline, so it's entertaining for people.'

But while the 'good girl goes bad' tag provided a perfect storyline for Middle America, it provided those Christians who saw Katy as having strayed from the Lord's flock with all the nails they needed to crucify her. In response, she told *The Advocate*, 'My platform in life isn't necessarily to preach. I respect everybody's faith. For me, honestly, it took a while to get to that point of respecting everybody's opinion. I was raised in a household where that wasn't necessarily allowed. There's no such thing as respecting everybody's faith in my kind of upbringing.'

'The fact of the matter is that girls, a lot of the time, smell much better than boys. We smell like vanilla. We smell like watermelon. We smell like strawberries. So, duh!' – Katy Perry

She also added: 'I'm in the business of rock'n'roll. I make mistakes. I'm human. I'm flawed. I accept that. I'm not here to preach the gospel right now other than to be a good f**cking musician.'

Having ripped away the scab, Katy continued: 'First of all, the song ["I Kissed A Girl"] is about an obvious curiosity. It's not about anything intense. The fact of the matter is that girls, a lot of the time, smell much better than boys. We smell like vanilla. We smell like watermelon. We smell like strawberries. So, duh! One day I was out with my boyfriend and I opened a magazine and realised, "You know what, honey? I would probably make out with Angelina Jolie if she wanted to." The song is about the beauty of a woman, and how that's changed a lot of things in life. It's started wars. It's ended wars. In general, it doesn't matter if you're female or male, if the right woman walks through the door; everybody's jaw is going to be on the floor.'

And Jason Flom's jaw would have hit Capitol Records' boardroom floor as 'I Kissed A Girl' topped the charts in twenty countries around the world – including a seven-week stint at the top of the *Billboard* Hot 100. In typically modest fashion, Katy, who was out on tour promoting the single when it claimed the *Billboard* top spot, would later say she couldn't remember where she was, or what she was doing when she heard the news she was Number One. 'I don't remember the specific city, but I knew we [soon] had a day off in Las Vegas, which was exciting because that is the best place to celebrate anything, right?' she later recalled. 'My producer sent me a bottle of Dom Perignon, and it showed up at the hotel. We took it and sat by the pool. We just raised our glasses and said, "How the hell did we do this?"'

Onto a winner: Katy with her award for Best International Female Solo Artist at the 2009 Brit Awards in London.

Pretty Pearls And Chapsticks

'I think there's a fine line between being a slut and being classy, I walk in-between that line.'

One Of The Boys – the sleeve of which featured a Vargas-esque Katy reclining on a sun-lounger in shorts and bustier – hit the shops on Tuesday, 17 June 2008, and the following week the album slammed onto the *Billboard* 200 at Number Nine, having sold over 47,000 copies.

In a review that was bound to have pleased Katy, *Billboard* magazine compared her to Alanis Morissette, stating 'Not since *Jagged Little Pill* has a debut album been so packed with potential hits.' While in a more temperate review, *Music OMH* – also acknowledging Katy's debt to Alanis ('from the feisty persona to the perky voice shifting octaves mid-syllable') – ultimately summed *One of the Boys* up as 'sparky and accomplished – though entirely disposable – pop.'

While in the US reviews were mixed, over in the UK the critics were rather more upbeat in their appraisals.

'So Katy Perry kissed a girl – we all know that, but what else has this feisty Californian singer – who cites Queen as her biggest influence – got to offer?' the BBC's Lizzie Ennever pondered when opening her review. The answer, she decides, is 'rawness', 'diversity', and an introduction to 'the real Katy'. Having made mention of how Katy identifies with her audience by singing about her own experiences, Ms Ennever goes on to credit Katy for managing to 'convey her emotions with a pretty varied and impressive vocal range'. She then attempts to pin Katy's sound down by making comparisons with three other pop princesses: 'She's got a sound that's kind of Cerys Matthews crossed with Avril Lavigne, but there's a modern, reborn-Britney-esque tinge, which keeps *One Of The Boys* sounding fresh and funky.'

Capturing the theatrical spirit of her work, *The Daily Telegraph* preferred to compare Katy to Disney's all-singing-all-dancing pop cultural phenomenon: 'With witty lyrics about partying ["Waking Up In Vegas"], and the trials and tribulations of the dating game ["If You Can Afford Me"], this is pure teen melodrama, a kind of deflowered college sequel to *High School Musical*.'

Grammy glamour: Katy arrives at the 51st Annual Grammy Awards in Los Angeles.

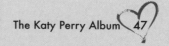

It's worth remembering that Katy's target audience – predominantly teenage girls from America's junior high schools – would have understood perfectly where Katy was coming from with the album title, as many of them would have grown up being considered 'one of the boys' until the boys in question noticed their tomboy buddy was wearing a training bra. 'It's a coming of age song [about] that summer between junior high and high school when all the girls suddenly grow and changed from being someone guys made fun of to being this Bambi-like creature that they wanted to be with,' Katy explained to *Tideline*. 'The girls grew, changed, developed, and all of a sudden the boys stopped trying to make fun of them and started wanting to be around the girls . . . because they looked pretty and smelled pretty.'

And then, of course, there was the tantalising taste of their cherry chapstick . . .

Following on from 'One of the Boys' and 'I Kissed A Girl' are the tracks 'Waking Up In Vegas' and 'Thinking Of You', both of which, of course, had played a pivotal role in Katy being picked up by Capitol. Though Katy could already boast of having had assistance from renowned songwriter Desmond Child when penning 'Waking Up In Vegas', Capitol brought in award-winning producer Andreas Carlsson, who'd worked with a diverse array of artists ranging from Britney Spears and The Backstreet Boys to Def Leppard and Bon Jovi, to add his own magic to the mix.

Specs-tacular: Katy attends a Betsey Johnson fashion show in New York.

Katy hadn't needed anyone's help whilst penning 'Thinking Of You', as it relates her break-up with Matt Thiessen. And whilst that period of her life wasn't a particularly happy one, it did have its positives. 'It's ["Thinking Of You"] probably the best representation of me [on the album] because I wrote it myself,' she told *Alloy*. 'It's a song that I think resonates in a lot of people's lives. It was a song I wrote being in a relationship and having to move on, not really necessarily wanting to move on in that relationship, but thinking I had to. And then finding myself with other people and hanging out with them, and feeling a really guilty feeling of cheating or something.'

Though 'Ur So Gay' was a tongue-in-cheek rant against guys who spent longer standing in front of the bathroom mirror on a Saturday night than she did, songs such as 'Hot N Cold' and 'If You Can Afford Me' showed that she wasn't willing to put up with lousy attitudes either. '["Hot N Cold"] is about a relationship. I was with this boy I really, really cared for, and we'd be having a conversation by text or by email and then he'd just disappear, for like three days,' she told *Digital Spy* of the song which would reach Number Three on the *Billboard* Hot 100 when released as a single. 'It would drive me crazy 'cause I would be like, "I thought we were making plans for this weekend?" I realised that this guy was the moodiest motherf**ker I ever met and honestly that's all it came down to. He changed moods like he was going through the menopause.'

'You know, guys don't get the picture that us women love them and that we love them eternally, and some younger guys don't get that we want consistency every once in a while,' she continued her theme with *Tideline*. 'I was seeing a guy who was definitely like, "Yeah, I'm gonna take you to dinner" – and for me, those words meant, "Shower. Shave. Everything. Nails. Dress. Feet." And then, all of a sudden, 8:00pm comes round and he's like out with his dudes and you're like, "Oh, my God, I just went through this whole transformation, and I HATE YOU! DO YOU KNOW HOW MUCH THIS MAKE-UP COSTS?!"'

'I'm eager to prove to people that, even though I'm a pop artist on a major label, I'm legit. I play my guitar and the band rocks, and I want to earn the respect of everyone out there.'
– Katy Perry

While she was desperate to be held by a real man, 'If You Can Afford Me' was a clear 'hands off' message to the alpha males who assumed that their splashing out for a bowl of pasta and a bottle of house red entitled them to breakfast. '"If You Can Afford Me" – that's about a girl being sassy to a guy – "It takes more than a wink, more than a drink."' She told *Metro Mix*. 'It's a weird thing, dating these days. In Hollywood, a guy asks a girl to go to dinner and thinks he's going to get something out of it. So the song is a message that says, "Please, I'm worth more than that."'

Time would indeed reveal Katy's true worth, but for the time being she would have suffer the slings and arrows – and poison pens – of outrageous fortune. The first of which came just three days after the album's release when she packed her guitar and embarked on the Warped Tour 2008.

At first glance, sending sugar-coated Katy out on the Warped Tour – a gruelling ten-week music and extreme sports tour, which was sponsored by footwear giants Vans, and specialised in bringing punk-related music to America's teenage masses – might seem a strange strategy. But what better way to prove yourself than having to vie for the audience's attention whilst ten other bands are strutting their respective stuff. But while roughing it playing in parking lots and fields didn't faze Katy in the least, she did have reservations about the tour being predominantly male-orientated. 'I'm really scared because there's a lot of boys on that tour and not a whole lot of women,' she explained to *AZ Central*. '[But] I also thought to myself: I'm a pop girl on a major label and I get the opportunity to do something as cool as the Warped Tour, and not have to open up for some lame-ass singer.'

As the tour – which was essentially a camping trip across America – lacked certain niceties, she posted the following SOS on her website: 'I'm scared because I heard that you don't get to shower every day, so I'll be bringing baby powder everywhere. If you're coming to the

Warped Tour, please bring me perfume bottles. It's going to be a lot of boys – a lot of smelly boys, [but] it's going to be a lot of fun. I'm excited.'

It was going to take a lot win over the skateboarding hordes, but unlike the vast majority of pretty pop singers clogging up the airwaves, Katy played a mean guitar. 'I'm eager to prove to people that, even though I'm a pop artist on a major label, I'm legit,' she explained. 'I play my guitar and the band rocks, and I want to earn the respect of everyone out there.'

And for any would-be detractors hoping to knock her off her stride, she chuckled: 'I wave and I say, "Hi, haters!" I smile really large, and then I laugh all the way to the bank!'

She added: 'I think that the Warped Tour is a challenge and a test for me. I am loading some of my own equipment. I'm walking the half-mile to the venue, just like everybody else. There's no golf-cart service. The humidity is hard to breathe in sometimes. There's dust. We get no soundcheck. If we can do this, I feel like I can probably do any tour.'

'I have bruises all over my legs. That's from wearing leggings. I'm jumping off the monitors and doing scissor-kicks, or trying to keep up with the boys.' – Katy Perry

And when *Rolling Stone* enquired how the girl whose album was sitting pretty in the *Billboard* 200 Top Ten was coping with the exertions of a rough and ready extreme sports tour, she was equally keen to show her battle scars. 'I have bruises all over my legs,' she told the magazine. 'That's from wearing leggings. I'm jumping off the monitors and doing scissor-kicks, or trying to keep up with the boys. It's funny, there's another stage going on right before I go on, and usually it's like a hardcore screamo band with a mosh pit spanning the size of the arena and I've got all pink gear and a soft pink bubblegum guitar. I definitely am keeping up with them, but I am causing injury at the same time.'

Although Katy bemoaned being out on the road with a busload of boys, the Warped Tour allowed her to get a little more intimate with the new man in her life, Travis 'Travie' McCoy, whose band, Gym Class Heroes was also on the bill. The couple, who shared the same producer, had first encountered each other a couple of months earlier at a Manhattan recording studio.

Katy has since gone on record as saying that although she doesn't fall in love often, when she does, she falls hard, but there initially didn't appear to be any magic in the air that afternoon. 'We didn't pay each other much attention because we were very focused on getting the songs done,' she told *Alloy*. 'But at the end of my trip – it was just when I first started going to New York and not really knowing anybody – I was like, "Please, God, somebody take me out." So I made him take me out.'

Travie, though instantly captivated by Katie's alpha-female stance, was himself too proud to initiate the first move: 'I was smitten as soon as she walked in the room,' he later said of first meeting Katy. 'She's a girl who demands attention. I have no game plan whatsoever, so I decided, "I'm just gonna ignore the s**t out of her."'

And having capitulated by making the first move, Katy then ceded much more to Travie by the time she returned to New York. They'd kept up their transcontinental romance whenever their studio schedules allowed, but spending ten weeks on the road together allowed them the necessary time to forge a more meaningful relationship. And the man-mountain Travie also came in handy when keeping unsolicited admirers at arm's length. 'My boyfriend is six-

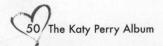

Katy's sassy pop wins over a skate-punk crowd during a performance on the Vans Warped Tour in Carson, California.

foot-five and covered in tattoos, so I don't get a whole lot of attention from [other] guys,' she chuckled to *Digital Spy*. 'They're pretty much scared s**tless!'

Whether her ex-beau Matt Thiessen, who was also on the Warped Tour bill with Relient K, was scared, Katy neglected to say, but their spending ten weeks in such close proximity must have made for the occasional uncomfortable moment. And then of course, there was also the fact of her going on stage every night performing 'Thinking Of You', and knowing that Thiessen was somewhere in the crowd.

With *One Of The Boys* continuing to sell like proverbial hotcakes, with each tour stop-off Katy slowly began to realise that her fame was preceding her. One example of this groundswell came during the Canadian leg of the tour. 'I was grabbing some food with my band at this restaurant. We were just eating and I noticed the waiters had this quote on the back of their shirts, and this quote said: "I've kissed more girls than Katy Perry,"' she told *Digital Spy*. 'It was the most random thing I've ever seen in my life! I was like, "What's happening? Who did this? Is this a joke? Am I being Punk'd right now?" When I see little things like that, I think, "What did I do?"'

What she was doing was slowly – and yet ever so surely – wowing America. Though she was the very antithesis of your typical Warped Tour act (in that she was a cutesy female pop singer with records doing very nicely on both the *Billboard* Hot 100 and the *Billboard* 200 charts, and who more often that not would take to the stage with a pretty pick parasol), the predominantly male, punk audiences were joining in with the choruses. 'I learnt so much on the Vans Warped Tour because I don't think the crowd was there to see me, so I really had to win them over every single show,' she later told *Company* magazine. 'That was cool, and I was happy to do that because fighting for their attention helped me get where I am today.'

It wasn't only the kids of America that were worshipping at the altar of Katy Perry, as the music industry's movers and shakers were beginning to sit up and take notice. And Katy returned to LA after the Warped Tour to learn that she'd been nominated for five awards – 'Best New Artist', 'Best Art Direction', 'Best Cinematography' and 'Best Female Video' for 'I Kissed A Girl' – at the 2008 Video Music Awards, which were set to take place in New York on Sunday 7 September. Though Katy would walk away empty-handed on the night, just being nominated in five categories was proof that she was finally being taken seriously. And while the awards gave her an opportunity to hook up with Travie, it was there that she would first encounter her future husband, Russell Brand.

> '**I met Russell Brand who I'm in love with. I love him, he's so great.**
> **He's got the worst sense of humour in the best sense of the way.' – Katy Perry**

The comedian, who was already a household name in Britain owing to his brash, in-your-face personality and risqué jokes, was hosting the VMA award ceremony as a means of raising his profile in America. And while Brand's zany humour was lost on a sizeable percentage of the audience, Katy was one of those who found his jokes hilariously funny – even the ones at her expense. But far from being offended, Katy had found herself warming to the comedian, and even accepted his invitation to make a cameo appearance in his forthcoming comedy movie, *Get Him To The Greek*. 'I met Russell Brand who I'm in love with,' she later told BBC Radio One. 'I love him, he's so great. He's got the worst sense of humour in the best sense of the way.'

Three days on from the glitzy VMAs, Katy embarked on a mini six-date European tour which saw her make her London debut at the Water Rats, situated in Kings Cross. While the Warped Tour had acclimatised Katy to playing the sort of places other female singers might fear to tread, 'I Kissed A Girl' was sitting pretty at Number One on the UK singles chart – and had been doing so for the past five weeks – and yet here she was strutting her stuff in front of just two hundred people in a venue that was little more than a West London pub with a live-music license.

The Guardian's Caroline Sullivan was in the crowd and opened her review with a flippant observation that playing a pub, rather than a theatre or an arena, ensured the gig was going to be a sell-out. But unfortunately for Katy, the comments didn't get any kinder: 'Although her ode to pretend lesbianism (it turns out she is a boy-kisser in real life) has made her a household name in the US, Perry does not yet have much to offer as a live performer.' And while lauding the curtain closer 'I Kissed A Girl' as a 'fantastic song', which Katy sang 'like a star', Sullivan ended her review with the question: 'Can Perry build the bond that will make her a long-term star rather than a transient starlet?'

The Evening Standard, however, though equally bemused by the choice of venue, was infinitely more impressed: '[Katy's] vibrant performance showed real star quality, and could win over a crowd ten times bigger than this one.'

She sells sea shells: Katy finds a novel way
to approach the stage in Vienna, Austria.

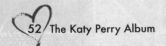

Some Like It Hot (N Cold)

'I've done a lot of bad things . . . use your imagination.'

While 'Hot N Cold' – the second single to be culled from *One Of The Boys* on Tuesday 30 September 2008 – failed to emulate its predecessor by claiming the coveted Number One spot on the *Billboard* 200, it did give Katy her second consecutive Top Three hit in the US and her second consecutive Top Ten hit in the UK. With the single also claiming pole position in Canada, Germany, Spain, and several other European countries, Katy unveiled plans for her mammoth, eighty-nine-date 'Hello Katy' headline world tour, which would see her performing in North America, Europe, Japan and Australia. The first ten-date US leg was set to commence at Seattle's 1,150-capacity Showbox at the Market on Friday 23 January 2009.

The tour poster showed an image of Katy peering suggestively over a slice of watermelon, which was obviously taken from the same photo-shoot as the image adorning the 'Hot N Cold' sleeve. But fruit, it seemed, was one of her guilty pleasures, as she revealed to *Billboard* magazine before embarking on the tour. 'I have the guy who creates stages for Madonna working on this tour; I'm indulging my obsession with fruit and cats, and designing all different outfits.'

When Katy arrived in Sydney on Friday 10 October for a show at the Entertainment Quarter, 'Hot N Cold' was riding high in the Australian chart. Following her second Australian date in Melbourne three days later, Katy then flew halfway around the world to appear at the Latin America MTV Awards in Guadalajara, Mexico, on Saturday 16 October, where she certainly left her mark, for instead of leaping onto a giant cake as a finale to 'I Kissed A Girl', she inadvertently slipped and crashed headlong into it. But the audience, thinking this was all part of the act, roared their approval.

Katy had been asked to host the European Music Awards to be staged at the *Liverpool Echo* Arena on Thursday 6 November, and British newspapers were still desperately keen to know if Katy really did enjoy kissing girls as much as she did boys – especially when it came to light that Katy had been snapped snogging an Agyness Deyn lookalike at the aftershow party following her London Scala show the previous September. 'Before you ask, the answer

All that glitters: Katy during a dress rehearsal for the Grammy Nominations Concert in Los Angeles.

is yes, I f**king kissed a girl!' she told *The Sunday Times Style* magazine. But though she was happy to admit to finding the female form arousing, she was quick to insist that her infatuation would never be anything more than a fantasy. 'I look at [girls] and think, "Oooh, I'm so turned on. What's happening?" . . . I'm attracted to cool, alternative women. But I'd only ever have a drink with them, I'm such a tease.'

Continuing her teasing banter about the possibility of her engaging in a same-sex relationship, she playfully told *Times Square Gossip*: 'If I could kiss anyone, it would be Miley Cyrus. She's the lucky girl.' She added: 'It's cool to hear through the grapevine that she has my song as her ringtone, although I think she's cheating on me. I think she might really go for it, we'll see. She's hosting the Teen Choice Awards, and I'll be on the show . . . maybe we'll have another Britney-Madonna moment onstage. How hilarious would that be? Although I don't think it would help her career. However, it would definitely help mine!'

One thing that was helping her career was that, with the world's press continually printing titillating tales about Katy kissing female members of her audience, it was guaranteed that a sizeable number of excitable males would be queuing up at the box office whenever Katy came to town.

Of course, if Katy chose to kiss girls in private that was her own business and no one else's, and if she was simply exploiting the male fascination with female erotica to maximise album sales, then there have been plenty of other singers who used similar tactics to achieve their goals. It's also possible that Katy, wanting something more substantial in her life than transcontinental trysts with Travie, had played up the 'does she, doesn't she?' gossip to force Travie's hand.

'I have the guy who creates stages for Madonna working on this tour; I'm indulging my obsession with fruit and cats, and designing all different outfits.' – Katy Perry

True, they had discussed marriage, and Travie had gone so far as to have her initials tattooed on his ring finger, but no amount of texts, phone calls and flowers was going to keep the flame alive with such a distance between them. They parted shortly into the New Year.

Cynics could also argue that Katy's career played some part in the split, as she was about to embark on a headline world tour, and her records were selling by the bucket-load, while 'Cookie Jar', the second single to be culled from Gym Class Heroes' album *The Quilt*, had stalled at a lowly Number 55 on the *Billboard* chart. That Travie took to posting caustic messages on his blog is evidence enough that the parting may not have been on the best of terms.

Of course, at the time of her split from Travie, Katy had been preoccupied with rehearsing for the forthcoming Hello Katy world tour. And whilst she'd penned 'Thinking Of You' as a means of putting closure on her relationship with Matt Thiessen, the irony of Capitol's decision to release that particular song as a single in advance of the tour wouldn't have been lost on her.

Despite many of the venues on the US legs of the Hello Katy Tour having sold out well in advance, and Capitol shelling out a considerable amount of cash for a promo video – presented as a flashback montage set during World War II, with Katy portraying a woman whose soldier-boy lover dies fighting for Uncle Sam – 'Thinking Of You' only just broke into the *Billboard* 200, and to date is the only Katy Perry single not to accrue seven-figure sales in the US.

Ahoy, sailor! Katy backstage during the filming of VH1 Divas Salute The Troops *in California.*

Though Katy had penned the song two years previously, its release as a single naturally brought it back to the fore. 'I wrote the song ["Thinking Of You"] after being in love for the first time,' she told *Cleveland.com*. 'None of that puppy love crap, but that "Okay, we're young adults, should we get married?" love. In the back of my mind, I had this slow-down yellow stop light that said, "I don't know if this is it. There's still a lot more things I want to try and accomplish in life!"'

She went on: 'I was really in love with this guy at the time, so it was really hard for me to move on. As I was moving on and meeting other people, he was constantly there in the back of my mind. I was comparing these new dudes to this old guy, my past relationship, and it wouldn't go away.'

'I Kissed A Girl' had been nominated in the 'Best Female Pop Vocal Performance' category at the 2009 Grammy Awards, which were staged in Katy's hometown, Los Angeles. While she deserved the prize for sporting an eye-catching outfit dripping with fresh fruit whilst performing the song on the night, she ultimately lost out to English singer/songwriter Adele's mournful 'Chasing Pavements'.

The European leg of the tour included three UK shows: the first at Manchester's O2 Academy on 25 February, followed by two London shows over consecutive nights at Koko in Camden Town. While Katy would have no doubt been looking forward to returning to the British capital, as with Katy's last visit to England, controversy was waiting for her – this time in the form of British pop sensation Lily Allen, who at the time was signed to Capitol Records.

'I'm not here to be a role model personality. I'm here to be in the business of rock'n'roll. Being in the business of rock'n'roll means having an attitude, being sexy, being edgy and being unapologetic.' – Katy Perry

The ongoing rivalry between Capitol's cuties had started several months earlier, when the oft-controversial celebrity gossip blogger Perez Hilton had posted a comment to the effect that Lily was peeved with her record label for shoving her aside and putting all their energies into promoting Katy. Lily had responded by saying Capitol was merely her American distributor, not her actual label, and that she herself had never heard of Katy Perry until reading Hilton's blog. Hilton, relishing having another celebrity raising to the bait, then published a photo of Lily posing with Katy, which suggested Lily was indeed miffed over Capitol's lavishing attention on Katy. And there the matter would have surely ended had not Katy – in one of those ill-judged moments – described herself on her Myspace page as being a 'fatter version of Amy Winehouse, and a skinnier version of Lily Allen'.

This innocuous comment would prove too much for Ms Allen, who at the time of Katy's arrival in the UK, was basking in the success of her second album, *It's Not Me, It's You*. After saying that she knew 'for a fact' that Capitol had signed Katy to be an American version of herself on the *popdirt.com* website, she ranted: 'It's like, [Katy] you're not English and you don't write your songs – shut up!'

Rather than get embroiled in a war of words with Lily, Katy opted to pour oil onto troubled waters. 'We are both quite different,' she told the press. 'She's got the cool, reggae, laidback sensibility with kooky lyrics and a great sense of humour. My stuff is a little more rock and pop, and somewhat more mainstream. I think we both have different things to offer. Is there

Left: Lollipopular: Katy wins over the studio audience during an appearance on the Today *show in New York.*
Right: Arriving at the Ed Sullivan Theatre for an appearance on The Late Show With David Letterman.

bad blood? Not from me. I will continue to buy her records. She's actually looking great these days, pretty fit.'

Though the 'Thinking Of You' single had proved something of a disappointment, on Tuesday 21 April, Capitol threw both caution and common sense to the wind by releasing 'Waking Up In Vegas' as the fifth single from *One Of The Boys*. And their faith in the song was rewarded when it climbed twenty places higher than 'Thinking Of You' on the *Billboard* chart, reached a very respectable Number 19 on the UK chart, and even claimed the Number One spot in Australia.

Aside from the accompanying promotional video, which was shot on location in Las Vegas, during which Katy got to race up and down the Strip in a $380,000 limited edition Lamborghini Murciélago, the single's chart placing was also helped by an appearance on *American Idol*, when she performed the song sporting a Vegas-era Elvis rhinestone jumpsuit.

Clothes had always been important to Katy, and getting to dress up in vintage outfits for the videos was great fun. For the 'Waking Up In Vegas' video Katy had donned vintage costumes provided by legendary fashion designer Bob Mackie, who in his career had dressed Judy Garland, Liza Minnelli, Diana Ross, Cher, and Tina Turner. Indeed, Katy was as excited about getting to wear Mackie's costumes as she was driving the Lamborghini 'I have to tell you one of my favourite things were those costumes,' she raved to *Clevelend.com*. 'They're from his [Mackie's] vintage collection. [They were] some costumes from the eighties and seventies. Who knows? Cher might have worn it.'

'I always wanted to share my story, and I wanted the world to sing along with my story.' – Katy Perry

The following month she wowed the diamond-studded crowd – which included ex-president, Bill Clinton – at the Life Ball in Vienna, the annual charity event designed to raise millions of dollars for AIDS and HIV sufferers, by wearing a daring, flesh-coloured mermaid outfit adorned with imitation starfish and various other sea creatures. According to *The Daily Mail*, the sparkling one-piece costume 'left very little to the imagination'.

Later that same month at the Video Music Awards staged in Saitama, Japan, Katy took to the stage in her most daring outfit to date. Midway through performing 'I Kissed A Girl' – for which she won the 'Best Pop Video' award – she pulled back her kimono to reveal a leotard embroidered with sushi. The press were probably pondering at what stage Katy would show up with nothing but a fig leaf covering her modesty, but whereas some female artists need to show off their assets to mask their musical deficiencies, Katy was just having a little fashionista fun.

And as Travie McCoy had accompanied Katy to Vienna for the charity bash, the press was also pondering if the couple had rekindled their romance. Travie certainly thought so, and was gushing to the assembled media about how he happy he was. But his happiness would prove short-lived, for Katy had her sights set on a Brand-new boyfriend . . .

Above and right: Katy proves that red is definitely her colour, onstage in Los Angeles and Miramar respectively.

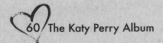

10

My Missing Puzzle Piece

*'I can't rate myself, but if you ask Russell
I'm sure he'd rate me ten out of ten.'*

Though Katy's cameo role in Russell Brand's latest movie *Get Him To The Greek*, in which the comedian reprises the character Aldous Snow from the 2008 movie *Forgetting Sarah Marshall*, would end up on the cutting-room floor, rehearsing the screen kiss with Brand that was required for the scene would lead to much, much more. For while it was perhaps to be expected that the Essex-born lothario would boast that having to express pleasure whilst kissing Katy hadn't required any acting, Katy herself also confessed to having enjoyed her time on screen. 'My scene called for me to make-out with him [Brand], and on the way down the stairs after the scene, I was hopping like a bunny,' she gushed. 'I hop like a bunny when I'm happy; I get a bit child-like. He gives me the Christmas Eve jitters.' And little could she have imagined that she'd be accompanying Brand to the movie's US premiere as his wife.

Katy's experiences on the set of *Get Him To The Greek* with her future lover/husband resulted in her penning 'Not Like The Movies', which would of course appear on her follow-up album *Teenage Dream*. 'I'd just gotten out of a relationship, and it wasn't how it is in the movies, so I was like, "But why can't it be?"' she later told *Company* magazine. 'I ended up finishing the song after I met someone [Brand] that made me finally feel, "This is magical." Your love life can have movie moments.'

But while Katy would certainly have loved to remain on the set to see what might happen between them, she had a world tour to be getting on with. Having said that, however, she knew hers and Russell's paths would cross again in the coming months as Brand – despite causing controversy at the previous year's ceremony by referring to then President George W. Bush as a 'retarded cowboy' – had been invited to host the 2009 MTV Video Music Awards in New York. And of course, having been denied the 'satanically' secular pleasures of MTV as a child, Katy was thrilled to be invited to the awards – regardless of whether she won anything. 'MTV is still really cool because it's so spontaneous. You never know what you're going to get,' she told *Company* magazine. 'And some of it is amazing; some of it's so crazy.

*Katy and her husband-to-be Russell Brand attend the
exclusive* Vanity Fair *Oscars party in 2010.*

My personality fits with that "you never know what you're going to get" type of vibe.'

Onlookers at the rehearsals for the awards at the Radio City Music Hall were left in no doubt that something was in the air as, after Katy had playfully bopped Brand – or Russell, as she now called him – over the head with a plastic bottle, the two proceeded to trade flirtatious insults.

As for the show itself, Katy performed a duet of Queen's 1977 hit 'We Will Rock You' with Aerosmith's Joe Perry, while 'Hot N Cold' lost out to Taylor Swift's 'You Belong To Me' in the 'Best Female Video' category. But Brand was determined that Katy wouldn't leave empty-handed and told the audience – not to mention all those viewing on television sets around the world – that as Katy hadn't won an award, and was staying in the same hotel as he was, he would be happy to provide a shoulder for her to cry on. 'So in a way,' he half-joked, 'I'm the real winner tonight.' Later that same night at Lady Gaga's aftershow party, whilst the hostess was entertaining her other A-list guests, Katy did indeed have her head nestled on Brand's shoulder. And needless to say, it wasn't sympathy she was after.

The following day, after the lovebirds had flown off to fulfil their respective commitments, Brand sent Katy a poem and – knowing she was a skilled song-smith – asked for something similar in return. But the mischievous Katy had a better idea and teasingly sent Brand a photo of her bare breasts with the word POEM scribbled across.

However, if the self-confessed sex addict thought the photo was a subliminal – open-ended – invitation into her boudoir then he was to be sorely disappointed. For though Katy agreed to go out for dinner with Brand that September (when the comedian presented her with a black diamond necklace and a copy of his autobiography, *My Booky Wook*), she made it plain there would be no 'afters' as she had no intention of becoming just another celebrity notch on the comedian's headboard. And while Katy described a spur-of-the-moment trip to Thailand with Russell as 'magical', the pair refused to confirm persistent press rumours that they were in a relationship.

But, of course, playful Katy had no intention of holding out indefinitely . . .

In October, Russell joined Katy in Paris, where she was catching up on the latest haute couture trends during Fashion Week. Whilst there, the couple took time out from getting to know one another to pay a visit Jim Morrison's grave at the city's celebrity cemetery, Père Lachaise. The Doors' hell-raising frontman had died from a suspected heroin overdose in 1971 – years before Russell and Katy were born – but to Russell, 'Mr Mojo', as the enigmatic Morrison had called himself, was the ultimate hedonist, while to Katy he was a fellow musician and a fellow Los Angelian.

Understandably, given the amount of time the two of them would have to spend apart, Katy wanted a man who she could trust to behave himself while she was out of his line of sight. And the serial seducer who once thought monogamy was a dark wood stunned Perez Hilton – along with other celebrity gossip columnists who thought it would never come to pass – by publicly declaring his love. 'I love Katy in a really pure way. She's a beautiful person, funny, gentle and sweet,' he gushed. 'But she's so demanding,' he added. 'A lot of the time, it's mental. She's a proper handful. It's very diverting. It's easy to be an arsehole, but now I've

Katy steps out with blue and purple highlights at
the MTV Video Music Awards in Los Angeles.

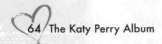

This blue wig became one of Katy's trademark looks during the California Dreams world tour.

found a woman who won't tolerate it.'

It appeared that he'd also found a woman happy to play to his fantasies, for having been invited to host that year's European Music Awards in Berlin on Thursday 5 November, midway through the proceedings Katy appeared on stage in a saucy claret and blue basque – the colours of Russell's favourite football team, West Ham United – complete with team crest and with his Twitter nickname, 'Rusty', emblazoned across the back of her hot pants.

By the end of the year Russell had relocated to Los Angeles, where he and Katy set up home together in a multi-million-dollar love-nest close to Griffin Park. And when Russell was subsequently 'papped' perusing jewellers' windows the rumour mill creaked into action.

Though items about an impending engagement announcement appeared in the celebrity gossip columns on a near-daily basis, it wasn't until the couple were enjoying a New Year break in Jaipur, India that Russell plucked up the courage to pop the question. Having already visited the Taj Mahal in Agra, and had matching Sanskrit script tattoos that translated as 'Go with the flow' inked on their inner arms, the lovers arrived in Jaipur – which to Katy's delight is popularly known as the 'Pink City' – where they checked into the luxurious Rambagh Palace Hotel to usher in the New Year. Russell, having secreted the ring within a bouquet of flowers, had obviously been waiting for the midnight chimes to propose, but never in his wildest dreams would he have expected to find himself doing so whilst sitting atop an elephant.

But that's exactly what happened, as following a romantic meal in the hotel's exquisite landscaped gardens, the couple were invited to watch a firework display from the back of an elephant. It must have been romantic but Russell would later quip, 'It's not a good idea to be on the back of an elephant during a fireworks display [as] they can't tell the difference between an apocalypse and New Year's Eve.'

2009 had undoubtedly been a good year for Katy. She'd undertaken her first headline world tour, played on the same stage as her heroine Gwen Stefani after being invited as a 'special guest act' on No Doubt's North American Summer Tour 2009, had scored another

'I like to have that food theme in everything I do,' Katy said. 'A candy theme!'

US Top Ten hit with 'Waking Up In Vegas', and was now engaged to be married. Her only fear now was what she was going to do to avoid 2010 being an anticlimax.

However, she needn't have worried . . .

The New Year – and new decade – got underway with Katy's second 'guest judge' appearance on *American Idol*, which was aired on the Fox network on Tuesday 26 January. Though the talent franchise was a worldwide phenomenon, if one were to take away the showbiz glitz, the TV cameras and studio audience, it wasn't so very different from what Katy had been doing to pay the rent at the Taxi Music offices before she got her own break. She could certainly empathise with the wide-eyed young hopefuls coming out on stage and giving their all, but with her own experiences of letdowns and hollow promises still fresh in her mind, she adopted the mentality that honesty would be the best policy.

Those finalists with a chance of winning the ultimate prize knew they could count on Katy's support, as she'd allowed two of her old songs, 'I Do Not Hook Up' and 'Slingshot', to feature on *All I Ever Wanted*, the latest studio album from the show's inaugural winner, Kelly Clarkson.

She also gave a helping hand to electro-hop duo 30H!3, one of the bands that had supported her on the Hello Katy Tour, by making a guest appearance on a remix of their latest single 'Starstrukk', as well as appearing in the promotional video. Despite her assistance the single stalled at 66 on the *Billboard* 200, but proved a surprise hit in the UK by claiming the Number Three spot.

One of her next projects possessed a modicum of shock value as she was invited to lend her voice to a new 3D movie, *The Smurfs*, a big-budget adaptation of an innocuous 1980s animated series which – for reasons known only to themselves – was one of the shows that had been placed on the Hudson family blacklist. 'I was never allowed to watch *The Smurfs*,' Katy wistfully told *The Toronto Sun*. 'Maybe it was very sorcery-based, or magical, or that Smurfette [her character] was the only female in the village – a slut, basically. Who knows? But can you imagine how my mother felt when I called up and said, "Hey, I'm a Smurfette!"'

The movie featured several live actors, including Neil Patrick Harris (best known for playing Doogie Howser M.D. in the early 1990s), and Hank Azaria, who rose to prominence providing numerous character voices in *The Simpsons* before coming front-of-house, so to speak, in movies such as *Along Came Polly*, *Run Fatboy Run*, and *Night At The Museum: Battle Of The Smithsonian*. The producers couldn't be accused of having purposely brought Katy onto the movie to cash in on her popularity, as they were unaware of whom the female voice they'd selected for the role of Smurfette belonged to. As Katy herself explained: 'They had done a blind test where they took certain voices from previous interviews and matched them with the character. They liked my voice without even knowing who it was. And when they found out it was me, they thought that would work out. My personality was just a plus!'

Of course, the Smurfs weren't the only TV characters that Katy would associate with, as she made cameo appearances on both *Sesame Street* and *The Simpsons*. Her cameo on *Sesame Street* would end up on the cutting-room floor, having been considered too provocative for younger viewers (the segment would, of course, subsequently appear on YouTube), but the censors surprisingly had no qualms about allowing Katy's appearance on *The Simpsons* to be broadcast on Sunday 5 December 2010. In the episode, 'The Fight Before Christmas', Katy appears wearing a low-cut, figure-hugging *Simpsons* motif dress, and having long been a fan of hugely successful cartoon, she was honoured to be invited onto the show, and considered it one of the 'highlights of my career' thus far.

However, while making guest appearances on various projects kept Katy in the public eye, her fans – not to mention the moneymen at Capitol Records – were pressing for a brand-new Katy Perry album in 2010.

Katy photographed in Sydney during a promotional tour in support of her album Teenage Dream.

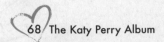

11

Let Your Colours Burst

'I've known that I wanted to be a musician since
the age of nine, and honestly, it's an amazing feeling.
I feel like if I continue to do things with integrity and always
nurture my core, then I think I could possibly win.'

One of the first new songs Katy wrote for the follow-up album was 'Teenage Dream', which would of course end up as the title track. 'I wrote that song in Santa Barbara, and it was a very pure moment for me because that's where I'm from,' she told *Celebuzz*. 'It was like, where I started my creative juices. Also, it kind of exudes this euphoric feeling because everybody remembers what their teenage dreams were – all the girls that were on your poster walls . . . and I want to continue to be one of those teenage wet dreams.' She expanded further on her website: 'That's such a great word, teenager. It is a very descriptive word; it packs a lot of emotion and imagery into three syllables. I couldn't believe after all of our agonising over "youth" themes, that we had overlooked such an obvious one – the teenage condition.'

The next song to be considered worthy of inclusion on the new album was 'Last Friday Night (T.G.I.F)'. 'There's nothing better than an impromptu dance party with my friends,' Katy explained to *Company* when asked about the song that would give her her sixth US Number One. '[It's] a song about debauchery because I had one of those nights in Santa Barbara. We went out to this place called Wildcat, and got crazy. We had a couple of beers and danced until we died, then brought the party back to the hotel room. Most of that song is actually truth, apart from the ménage-à-trois . . . unfortunately! But, yes, streaking in the park, that's what we did, so we had to write a song about it.'

One song which almost didn't make the final track-listing was 'Peacock'; as Jason Flom and Capitol's other execs were anxious about its sexual innuendos. While they were happy for Katy to sing about kissing girls and liking it, not-so-veiled allusions to the male genitalia such as 'I wanna see your pea-cock, cock, cock', and 'let me see what you're hiding underneath', were considered too risqué. 'They [Capitol] were all a bit worried about the word "cock" and it gave me déjà vu because they did exactly the same thing with "I Kissed A Girl,"' she later recalled. 'They said, "We don't see it as a single, we don't want it on the album." And I was like, "You guys are idiots."'

*Peacock plumage: One of Katy's more elaborate costumes gets an airing
during the North American leg of her California Dreams tour.*

Although Katy was predominantly targeting school and college kids the world over, she wasn't afraid of penning the occasional introspective song. For though 'Pearl' started out being about an imaginary woman, she quickly realised she was writing about herself. 'It's the story of a person who changes because of a relationship,' she told *Cool!* magazine. 'She was a pearl and now, she is just a shadow of herself because she let the other person destroy her. I've been inspired by all the women who lose sight of who they really are because of their relationship. It happened to me too! Since I've found my soulmate, I began to think about all the boys I've been with in the past and wondered why I sacrificed a part of me for some of them when I could have used this time to grow up and get to know myself.'

Another song which subliminally hinted at her newfound happiness was 'E.T', featuring rapper Kanye West on guest vocals. '"E.T." is a metaphor about finding someone who is just obviously not from this world, because how could they love me like this?' she subsequently told *Company* magazine. 'Even though it's a metaphor, I'm very interested in all things futuristic. I mean, I complain every day that the Hoverport has still not been invented! I look out into the sky and to the stars, and I feel there is so much out there.'

Getting back to what motivates her songwriting, she added: 'I focus on the lyrical side of things because I think words are so important. One of my favourite songs is Nick Cave's "Are You The One That I've Been Waiting For?" which ended up being engraved on the inside of my engagement ring.'

'I couldn't believe after all of our agonising over "youth" themes, that we had overlooked such an obvious one – the teenage condition.' – Katy Perry

Ultimately, it would be the final song which Katy wrote for the new album, 'California Gurls', that Capitol chose to release as the introductory single on 11 May. Unable to shake the feeling that her latest opus wasn't quite complete, she texted Chris Anokute asking him to hold fire on the track-listing as she was writing a new song about Californian girls. Anokute later recalled, 'At the time the Jay-Z song "Empire State Of Mind" was huge, and everyone in LA was singing "New York . . ." and she [Katy] wanted to have a song for California. She had the whole vision.'

Katy subsequently admitted as much herself to MTV Asia: 'I was hearing about "Empire State Of Mind", and I was jealous! What about California? What about The Beach Boys, or Tupac [Shakur]? I thought it would be time for a West Coast anthem with my twist. It's my favourite video that I got to make. I was eating real cotton-candy, and I was like, "That's not work! That's play!"'

About the song itself, she added: 'When you hear the song, you think, "Girls on the beach, in bikinis and next-to-nothing," the same treatment you've seen for a lot of different music videos. I think it was just time to step up my game and the whipped-cream breasts were all a part of it.'

'I decided to use my best assets,' she cheekily said to camera during a break whilst filming the video. 'Put some whipped-cream on them, and spray those Gummy Bears!' It would soon be champagne foam spraying around Jason Flom's office at the Capitol Records Building when 'California Gurls' gave Katy her second US Number One. It claimed the top spot in ten

Far-East fashions: Katy's oriental styling and hot-pink hair ensured she was the centre of attention at the 2011 MTV Video Music Awards.

other countries around the world and was still sitting pretty at the top of the *Billboard* chart when Katy and legendary rapper Snoop Dogg performed the song live at the MTV Movie Awards on 6 June.

A further hint of just how massive the parent album was going to be came at the end of July when 'Teenage Dream' gave Katy her third US Number One single. The accompanying promo video was shot in Santa Barbara, where Katy's own teenage dream had begun, and featured many of her old school friends. And as all the pundits were predicting, when the album was released on 24 August it slammed onto the *Billboard* Hot 100 at Number One, selling 192,000 copies in the first week.

Though the album inevitably had its critics, with some attacking the 'Frankenstein-like' production, and labelling Katy's vocals 'robotic' and devoid of 'elegance and nuance', she did have her champions. The *LA Times* hailed *Teenage Dream* a 'great ad campaign [. . .] with hooks that hit like paintballs and choruses that exhort like slogans; she delivers them with the gusto of a pitchwoman.' *Rolling Stone* opined: '*Teenage Dream* is the kind of pool-party-pop gem that Gwen Stefani used to crank out on the regular.' It also felt the new album was 'superior in every way to *One of the Boys*', and praised her 'clever songwriting'. Of course, Katy's fans continued to champion their pop princess, and when the single 'Firework' was released on 26 October, it gave Katy her fourth US Number One.

Think pink: Katy at the American Music Awards in Los Angeles.

Of course, by the time 'Firework' was released, Katy and Russell had created plenty of sparks of their own by tying the knot in India on 23 October, in what has to be one of the most extravagant weddings ever staged. For though they'd bucked the celebrity trend by shunning multi-million offers from the likes of *Hello!* and *OK!*, preferring a private ceremony in the company of their nearest and dearest, the affair was anything but low-key; the lavish reception held at the Aman-i-Khás Hotel, close to Ranthambore's tiger sanctuary, allegedly included a parade of elephants, camels and horses, and possibly wafts of Katy's soon-to-be-launched perfume, Purr, drifting across the balmy air.

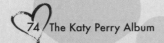

'I think "Last Friday Night (T.G.I.F)" will go down well with college kids because they're always learning by default – by hangover – but they somehow can never stop!'
– Katy Perry

And though the ceremony was conducted by a Christian minister at the behest of Katy's parents, Katy went out of her way to ensure that certain aspects – such as having her pal, gay fashion designer Markus Molinari as her bridesmaid – didn't follow convention.

Though Katy failed to pick up any of the three awards she'd been nominated for at the American Music Awards in November 2010, or any of the four awards she'd been nominated for at the 2011 Grammys in February – where she performed 'Not Like The Movies' and 'Teenage Dream' – this disappointment would soon be forgotten as 'E.T.' claimed the top spot on the *Billboard* 200 following its release later that same month.

Having a fifth US Number One should have seen Katy in seventh heaven, but according to reports, Katy and Russell were experiencing difficulties just five months into their marriage. Aside from the usual problem of their respective career commitments keeping them apart, Katy was believed to have been upset by Russell having posted a photo of her *sans* make-up on his Twitter page. Indeed, *Life & Style* went so far as to claim Katy and Russell were seeking marriage counselling. However, Katy was quick to quash the rumours by telling

At the 2011 MTV VMAs, where she was nominated for ten categories and won Video of the Year, for 'Firework'.

Gossip Cop that 'everything was great' between herself and Russell. And on her own Twitter page, in an oblique reference to the rumours, she paraphrased a line from Shakespeare's *Henry IV* by saying: 'Heavy is the head that wears the crown, don't let the greatness get you down.'

Unfortunately for Katy, rumours of marital strife persisted in the gossip columns. So much so, that a couple of months later she again elected to tweet her discontent: 'Just because we don't flaunt our relationship doesn't mean there's something wrong with it. Privacy is our luxury. Tabloids are trash, gossip is gross.' Hubby Russell added: 'You tell 'em Mrs Brand! In Britain we're currently dismantling the scum media so I'm not tuned in to their brain-farting.'

Whatever the truth about her marriage, Katy's career at least was going strong. To promote *Teenage Dream*, Katy unveiled plans for her 122-date California Dreams Tour. The world tour, which would commence with a show at the Campo Pequeno in Lisbon, Portugal on 20 February 2011, would take in North America, Europe, Australasia, Asia, and South America, and earn Katy a staggering $26 million. 'This show is a big production,' Katy told *Company*, 'but there will be wonderful moments where I can strip it down to just me and my guitar. Yes, people will be able to dance and maybe they will be able to cry, but in a lovely way. And, I don't want to ruin any surprises but I might be changing [costumes] over twenty times in one show.'

And the candy confetti was falling during the US leg of the California Dreams Tour, for on the eve of the tour Capitol had released 'Last Friday Night (T.G.I.F)'. It would prove a most prescient piece of marketing, as the single topped the US Billboard chart making it a grand slam of five US Number One singles from the same album, and earning Katy a lasting place in Billboard's illustrious history in the process. (The only other artist to achieve five Number Ones from the same album is Michael Jackson.)

'When you hear "California Gurls", you think, "Girls on the beach, in bikinis and next-to-nothing," the same treatment you've seen for a lot of different music videos.' – Katy Perry

The first leg of the tour took Katy to Portugal, Italy, Switzerland, Germany, Austria, France, Belgium, Netherlands, UK and Ireland, where she was greeted by a full house at every performance. From Europe, Katy moved on to Australasia, where it was a case of 'move over Kylie'. Following on from there and Japan, Katy returned to the US for a second mammoth forty-five-date North American leg, which would see her perform three shows in LA and two in her hometown, Santa Barbara. 'Perry was all charm and nonstop energy, [and] sounded fantastic from start to finish,' MTV said of Katy's 17 June show at the Nassau Veterans Memorial Coliseum in Uniondale, New York. 'She encored with "California Gurls", but the show's banner moment came at its official end with "Firework". With every person in the arena on their feet, Perry said, "I wrote this song for anyone who ever needed a song. To help them, to lift them up." And then she did exactly that. The Coliseum shook as the crowd sang the ubiquitous hit along with her as pyro lit up the stage, raining down like a wall of sparklers.'

After taking in shows in Brazil and Argentina, Katy kick-started the second European leg of her world tour with a show at Sheffield's 13,500-capacity Motorpoint Arena on 12 October. After wowing sell-out crowds in London, Liverpool, Cardiff, Belfast, Birmingham, Newcastle and Aberdeen, with an impressive nineteen-song set-list and lavish *Wizard Of Oz/Alice In Wonderland*-themed stage settings, Katy trick *and* treated her fans to something extra special at her Halloween show at Manchester's MEN Arena. 'Covered in sweets, candyfloss and enormous lollipops, the stage looked like it had come straight out of Willy Wonka's chocolate factory,' *The Manchester Evening News* enthused. 'But Katy also had a few tricks up her sleeve, blasting jets of foam onto her unsuspecting audience and coming out with an array of cheeky innuendos [...] As the show progressed, Perry proved she was more than just a pop gimmick, belting out hit after hit with a powerful voice. She danced tirelessly around the stage thrilling the audience with her lively performances of "Teenage Dream", "I Kissed A Girl" and "Last Friday Night". She even worked her way through at least six outfits while performing "Hot N Cold", slipping behind a curtain for a matter of seconds before unveiling another ensemble.

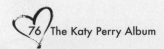

Left: *Catnipped! Onstage in Florida.* **Right:** *Katy goes back to her natural-blonde roots (with a hint of pink) at a 2011 benefit in Los Angeles.*

'It wasn't only Katy's pop anthems that kept the audience on their feet, as her slower numbers, notably "The One That Got Away", a cover of Adele's "Someone Like You", and "Thinking Of You", which she performed on acoustic guitar whilst hanging suspended on a candyfloss cloud, were enthusiastically received.'

On 20 November, Katy took time out to attend the American Music Awards, in which she'd been nominated in three categories including Artist of the Year. And though she lost out to Adele in all three, she did at least walk away from the Nokia Theatre with a special achievement award for being the first female singer to accrue five Number One singles from the same album.

Following a show in Oakland the following evening, Katy fulfilled her 2011 touring commitments with two sell-out hometown shows at the 20,000-capacity Staples Centre, where she once again took her audience on a 'neon-coloured journey through a twisted Candyland fairytale'. With the addition of two last-minute Asian dates for January 2012, the California Dreams Tour – ranked thirteenth on *Billboard*'s annual 'Top 25 Tours' of 2011 – will see Katy break the $50-million barrier, but behind the glitzy, bright-eyed smiles, all wasn't well with the Brand-Perry union. Alas, the continuing reports of problems with Katy's and Russell's marriage were not without substance. The gossip columns started setting their sights in earnest when instead of being with Katy in Belfast helping her celebrate her twenty-seventh birthday as she had initially planned, Russell was 3,000 miles away in New York, having inexplicably booked a series of last-minute stand-up shows. And though they were together for their first wedding anniversary, it was – according to a close friend – only because Katy had made the effort by booking a flight to New York before having to return to Belfast alone.

Further grist was added to the incessant rumour mill when Katy and Russell were snapped on opposite US seaboards *sans* wedding rings. And despite having publicly dismissed rumours on *The Ellen DeGeneres Show* at the beginning of December that he and Katy were planning to go their separate ways, which was followed the next day by a public outing at a benefit for the David Lynch Foundation, a few days later Katy alerted the Twitter twitchers by blithely mocking Russell's East London accent whilst impersonating her husband during a sketch on *Saturday Night Live*. And when reports that the supposedly happy couple had spent Christmas on different continents – Russell was in Cornwall on the English Riviera, while Katy was 7,000 miles away partying hard with friends in Hawaii – hit the newsstands, confirmation of what has to be one of Hollywood's worst-kept secrets came on 30 December, when it was announced Russell had filed for divorce citing grounds of 'irreconcilable differences'.

Katy reportedly asked Russell to file for divorce papers (in which she appears as Katheryn Elizabeth Hudson) because divorce goes against her religious beliefs. The papers – case no. BD556634 – also show there to be 'community property assets', suggesting the couple had forgone the formality of a pre-nup before jetting off to India to take their vows. If this is the case, then under Californian law Russell will be entitled to half of Katy's estimated $35-million fortune.

'This show is big, but there will be wonderful moments where I can strip it down to just me and my guitar. Yes, people will dance and maybe they will be able to cry, but in a lovely way.' – Katy Perry

According to 'sources close to the former couple', *The Sunday Mirror* revealed that Russell had filed for divorce from Katy because they'd fallen out over the idea of starting a family. On the aforementioned *Ellen DeGeneres Show*, Russell had said that he wanted to have children, which on the surface appeared to reinforce Katy's comments on the same talk show the month before, when she'd declared that she'd 'love to have children', and that if childbirth didn't hurt the first time she'd 'keep popping them out'. And appearing on ABC's *Most Fascinating People of 2011*, when host Barbara Walters asked Katy if she planned to have children, she replied: 'Yes of course, I think that is one of the biggest reasons why you do get married.' Yet with Katy navigating her way to the finale of a hugely successful world tour, and with 'The One That Got Away' sitting pretty at Number Three on the *Billboard* Hot 100, settling down to be a 'Hollywood housewife' was not on her immediate agenda. While Russell was beginning to make a name for himself in America, Katy herself was in a different league.

Insiders told the paper that, while Katy and Russell were keeping up a public pretence that they were happy together, their lawyers were working away in the background and had on two separate occasions come close to releasing an official statement explaining that the estranged couple were spending some time apart, only for Katy and Russell to pull back from the brink at the eleventh hour. Those closest to Russell had been growing increasingly concerned that he and Katy were woefully unsuited to each other, and that it would all end in tears once reality had kicked in.

The friend's chief concern – aside from the couple's hectic schedules keeping them apart – was Russell's inability to cope with Katy's partying now that her tour was coming to an

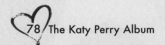

Katy preaches the California Dreams gospel in Tampa, Florida.

end. The Russell of old would have surely matched her drink for drink, but living with the knowledge that another fall from the sobriety wagon might kill him had slaked his thirst.

It's believed that Katy – having bowed to Russell's wishes to get away from LA for the festive break – had planned to hire a private plane to jet her family over to England so that they could all celebrate Christmas together, only to amend her plans in favour of a Hawaiian luau following what was subsequently reported as a 'massive fight' with Russell in the week prior to Christmas. Katy reportedly attempted to call her hubby's bluff by handing back her wedding ring, but if so, the bluff backfired, as he saw it as the final straw and decided to call time on their fourteen-month marriage.

While Katy's management have so far chosen to remain tight-lipped about the split, after having instructed his lawyers to file divorce papers with the Los Angeles Superior Court, Russell – who was still in London – said in a statement: 'Sadly, Katy and I are ending our marriage. I'll always adore her and I know we'll remain friends.'

Whether the mooted 'differences' will prove irreconcilable remains to be seen, but what is certain, however, is that there'll be more headlines, as well as records, world tours – and possibly even more Purr-fumes, before Katy decides it's time to put away her guitar.

Copyright © 2012 by Plexus Publishing Limited
Published by Plexus Publishing Limited
25 Mallinson Road
London SW11 1BW
www.plexusbooks.com

British Library Cataloguing in Publication Data

O'Shea, Mick.
    The Katy Perry album.
    1. Perry, Katy. 2. Women singers–United States–
    Biography. 3. Singers–United States–Biography.
    I. Title
    782.4'2164'092-dc23

ISBN-13: 978-0-85965-481-4

Cover and book design by Coco Wake-Porter
Printed in Great Britain by Scotprint

Acknowledgements
Thanks to Sandra, Laura and Tom at Plexus for their
assistance in my bringing the book in on time, Rupert
Tracy, and Jackie and Richard at P-PR. Thanks also to
Tasha 'Bodacious Babe' Cowen and Shannon 'Mini-
Hepburn' Stanley, for keeping the tea flowing, and
putting up with my mood-swings and frustrations
when occasionally stumbling over the dreaded writer's
block, Paul Young (not the singer) Lisa 'T-bag' Bird,
Johnny Carroll, Fi Bartlett and the twins, Debbie
Mustapha, Zoe Johnson-Meadows, Martin and Angela
Jones, Phil and Nic Williams.

    Katy Perry has given interviews to many
newspapers, magazines, websites, TV and radio shows,
and these have proved invaluable in chronicling her
life and career. The author and editors would like to
give special thanks to: *The Mirror; The Daily Telegraph;
Rolling Stone; BBC Entertainment; Prefix* magazine*;
CBS News; The Daily Mail; Blender* magazine;
*The Oregonian; Christian Music Central; Christian
Retailing; Philstar; Cross Rhythms; Star Pulse; Artist
Direct; BlackBook* magazine; *The Guardian; Bravo;
Christian Contemporary Music; Effect Radio; The
Star Scoop; The Scotsman; Seventeen; Stepping Out*
magazine*; Christianity Today; INK19; E! Entertainment;
Entertainment Weekly; Tideline; Hit Quarters; OMH
Music; Diva* magazine*; Buzznet; Metro Mix; BBC News;*
The *Times; The Advocate; The London Paper;
Q* magazine*; AllMusic; NME; Uncut* magazine*; Alloy;
Monsters and Critics; Digital Spy; AZ Central; Chron*
magazine*; Company* magazine*; BBC Radio 1; Beliefnet;
The Evening Standard; The Sun; NOW* magazine*; YRB*
magazine*; The Sunday Times' Style* magazine*; Times
Square Gossip; Cleveland.com; Glamour* magazine*; The
Toronto Sun; Celebuzz; Cool!* Magazine; *The LA Times;
Life & Style; Gossip Cop; Nova FM; The Sheffield
Telegraph; The Manchester Evening News;
The Sunday Mirror.*

    We would like to thank Delilah Walker-Coleman
and Pepe Balderrama for photo research and the
following agencies for supplying photographs: Corbis/
Stephane Cardinale/People Avenue for the cover
photograph; Mike Coppola/ FilmMagic/ Getty
Images; Gary Gershoff/ WireImage/ Getty Images;
Katy Perry's Official Twitter Page; Dos Pueblos High
School Yearbook; Mark Sullivan/ WireImage/ Getty
Images; Frazer Harrison/ Getty Images; L.Cohen/
WireImage/ Getty Images; Florian Seefried/ Getty
Images; Neilson Barnard/ Getty Images; Jason Meritt/
FilmMagic/ Getty Images; Alberto E. Rodriguez/ Getty
Images; Jesse Grant/ Getty Images; Startraks Photo/
Rex Features; Jeff Kravitz/ FilmMagic/ Getty Images;
AFP/ Getty Images; Bryan Bedder/ Getty Images;
Robyn Beck/ AFP/ Getty Images; Kevin Mazur/
WireImage/ Getty Images; Scott Legato/ FilmMagic/
Getty Images; Samir Hussein/ Getty Images; Katy
Winn/ Getty Images for IMG; Newspix/ Rex Features;
Jim Trifyllis/ Rex Features; Jeff Fusco/ Getty Images;
Eamonn McCormack/ WireImage/ Getty images;
Jon Kopaloff/ FilmMagic/ Getty Images; Stephen
Lovekin/ Getty Images; Stephen Albanese/ Getty
Images; George Napolitano/ FilmMagic/ Getty Images;
Michael Tran/ FilmMagic/ Getty Images; Matt Baron/
BEI/ Rex Features; Newspix/ Rex Features; Jim Smeal/
BEI/ Rex Features; Newspix/ Rex Features; Newspix/
Rex Features; Kristian Dowling/ Getty Images; Steve
Granitz/ WireImage/ Getty Images; Sipa Press/ Rex
Features; Tommaso Boddi/ FilmMagic/ Getty Images.

    Every effort has been made to acknowledge and
trace copyright holders and to contact original sources,
and we apologise for any unintentional errors which
will be corrected in any future editions of this book.